Contents

Use with *United States History*

UNIT 5 THE NEW NATION

UNIT 6 THE CIVIL WAR

UNIT 7 LINKING TO TODAY

ii

Use with *United States History*

Almanac Map Practice

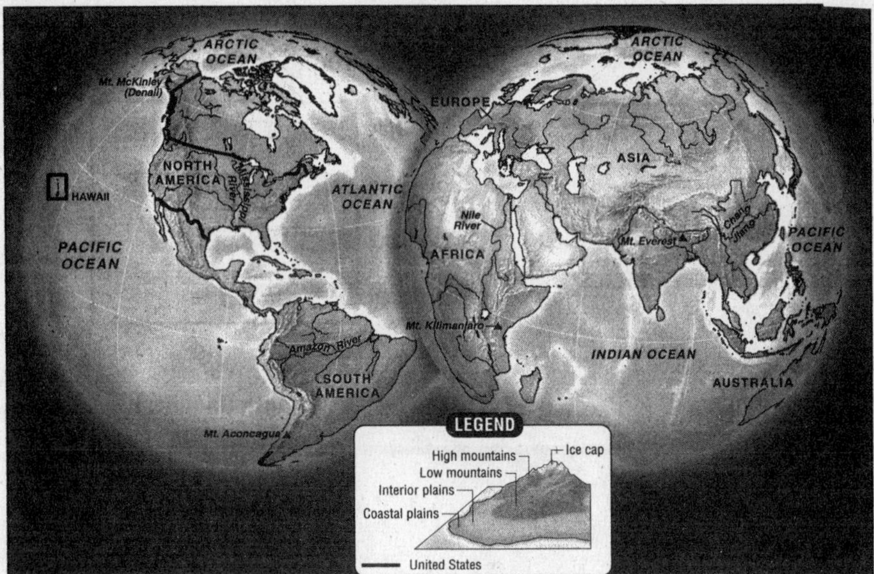

Use the map to do these activities and answer these questions.

Practice

1. Shade in Australia.

2. Which continent borders the Arctic and Indian oceans? ____________

3. Which mountain is farther south, Mt. McKinley or Mt. Kilimanjaro?

____

4. Use directional terms to compare the flow of the Amazon River to the

flow of the Mississippi River. _____________________________________

____

5. Draw a box around the mountain range along the western edge of
South America.

Apply

6. Read the first two paragraphs on page 39 of Chapter 2. Compare the
information in the paragraphs to the map above. Does Beringia still
exist? How can you tell?

____

____

____

    1   Use with *United States History*, pp. 2–3

Almanac Graph Practice

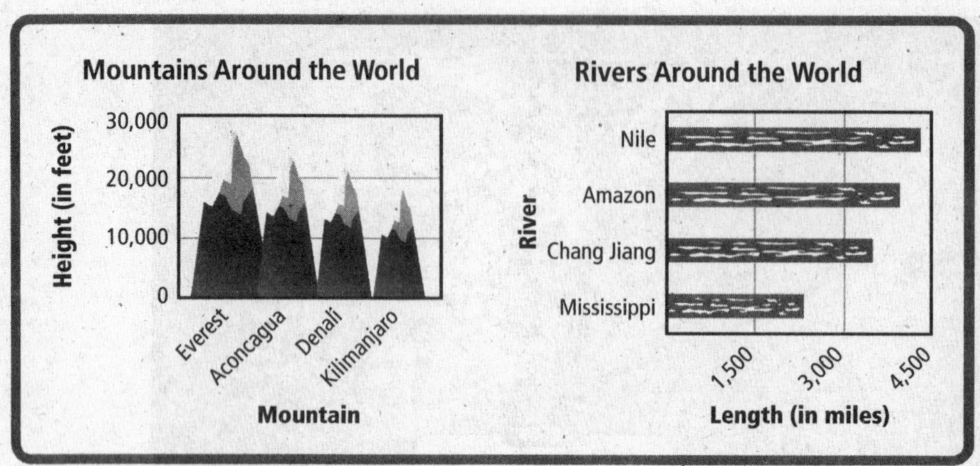

Practice

1. Name the river that is longer than the Mississippi River but shorter than the Amazon River. ____

2. About how many feet high is Mt. Kilimanjaro?

____

Apply

3. Use the information below to complete the bar graph.

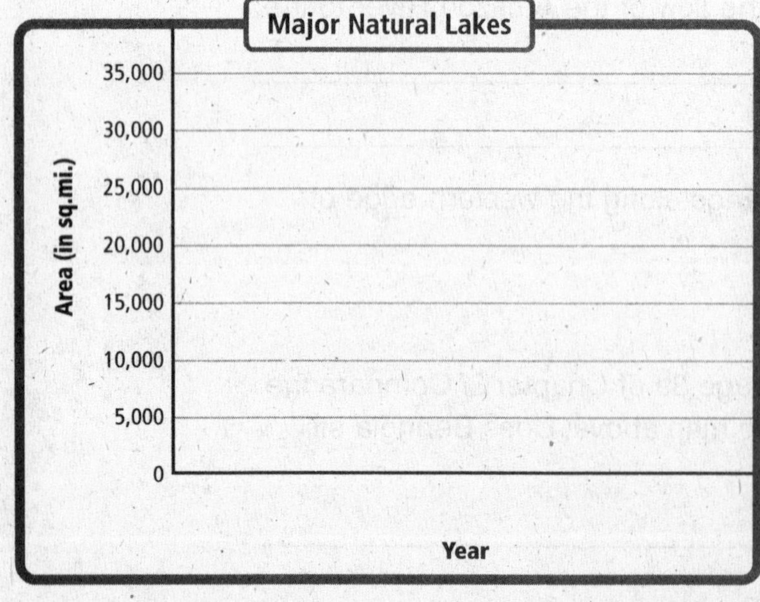

Major Natural Lakes

Lake	Area (in sq. mi.)
Superior	31,700
Victoria	26,828
Aral Sea	13,000
Great Bear	12,028
Nyasa	11,430
Erie	9,910

Use with *United States History*, pp. 2–3

Vocabulary and Study Guide

Vocabulary

After you read the section, fill in the word web.

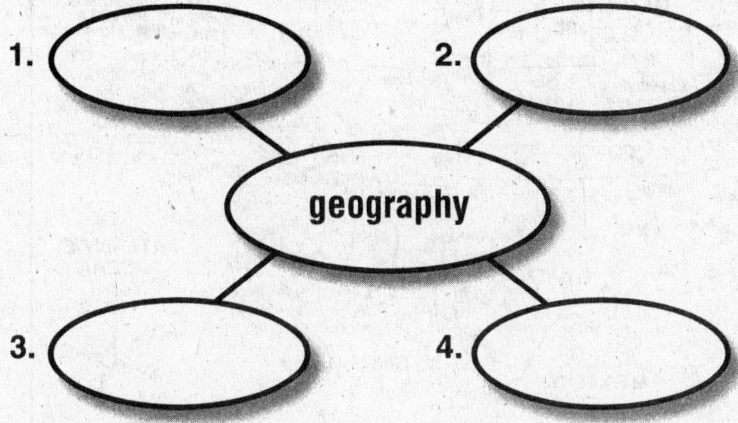

Study Guide

Read "A Varied Land." Then answer the questions.

5. What is geography?

____

____

6. What feature makes up part of the U.S. border with Canada?

____

7. What feature makes up much of the U.S. border with Mexico?

____

Read "Landforms." Then number the U.S. landforms in order from the West Coast to the East Coast.

8. Appalachian Mountains ___

9. Rocky Mountains ___

10. Sierra Nevada range ___

11. Grand Canyon ___

12. Atlantic Coastal Plain ___

13. Mississippi River ___

CHAPTER 1

Skillbuilder: Review Map Skills

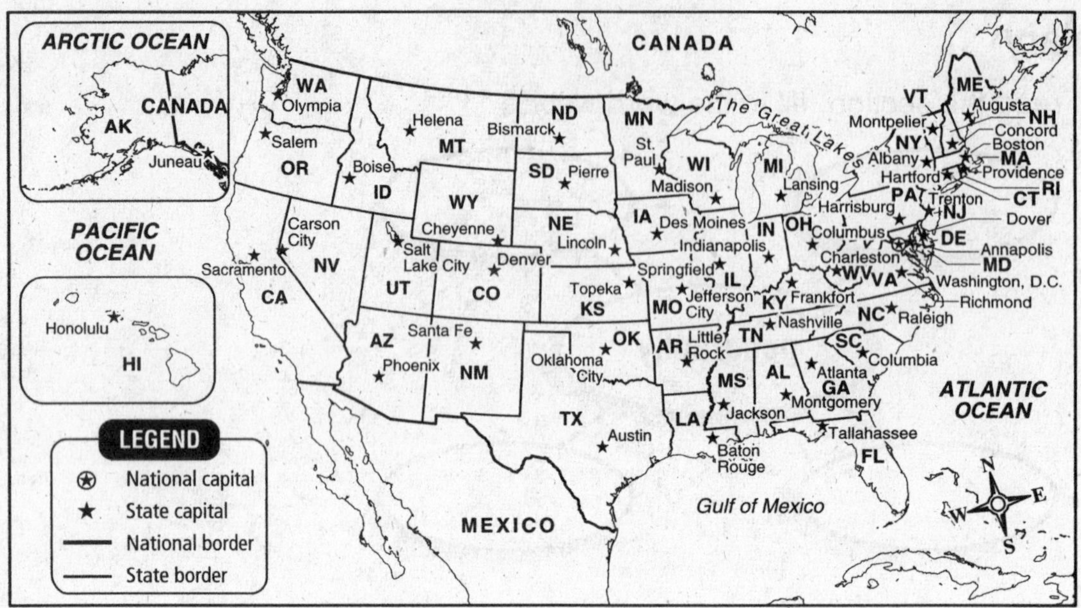

Practice

1. Circle the legend on the map. What symbols does the legend show?

____

2. To get from Austin, Texas, to Albany, New York, which direction would

you travel? ____

3. Which states share borders with Mexico? _____________________

____

Apply

Look at the natural resources map in Lesson 2. Find the region where
you live. Write the name of your state and two resources that come from
your region.

____

____

Vocabulary and Study Guide

Vocabulary

Write the definition of each vocabulary word below.

1. capital resource _______________________________________

____

2. human resources _______________________________________

____

3. conservation _______________________________________

4. scarcity _______________________________________

____

5. opportunity cost _______________________________________

____

6. Use two of the words in a sentence.

____

____

Study Guide

Read "Natural Resources." Then fill in the barrels below with examples of resources for each category.

Renewable	Nonrenewable	Flow
7.	8.	9.

10. Read "Other Important Resources." Then fill in the blanks below.

The tools, machines, and buildings that people use to make

goods are called _______________________. The skills and knowledge

that people bring to their work are called _______________________.

Vocabulary and Study Guide

Vocabulary

Solve the clue and write the answer in the blank. Then find the word in the puzzle. Look up, down, forward, and backward. Look for a bonus word!

1. An area that has one or more features in common _______________
2. The buying and selling of goods _______________
3. A person who buys goods and services _______________
4. Specialization helps each region make more of this _______________

Bonus Word:

A	D	O	K	P	T	S	G
E	Y	J	E	D	A	R	T
C	H	E	C	N	E	E	K
O	F	U	N	G	U	M	O
N	X	B	I	O	H	U	C
O	W	O	P	Q	M	S	T
M	N	C	M	V	K	N	H
Y	F	Z	Y	U	B	O	P
I	L	O	S	M	A	C	Q

Study Guide

Read "What Is a Region?" Then answer the questions.

5. Why do geographers divide areas into regions?

____

6. What are some ways to divide an area into regions?

____

____

7. Read "Regions and Resources." Then fill in the blanks below.

A region's resources are important for the growth of that region's _____________. The type of _____________ a region has helps that region's farmers decide which _____________ to grow. Certain regions specialize in certain crops, such as _____________ in the South and _____________ in the northern plains states. To increase the variety of available products, _____________ exists among regions.

Vocabulary and Study Guide

Vocabulary

Write each vocabulary word or phrase in the correct column.

harms the environment	erosion	pollution	ecosystem

Natural force	Human activity
1.	2.

Study Guide

3. Read "How Land Affects People." Then fill in the blanks below.

People settle in places where they are able to ______________.

A city's resources and its ______________ help its economy and

______________ grow. People also choose where they want to live

based on geography or the ______________. Some people live close

to mountains or lakes because they enjoy certain ______________.

Read "Changing the Land." Then fill in the chart below to show how
human activities can affect ecosystems.

Vocabulary and Study Guide

Vocabulary

Across
1. Another word for farming
2. An organized system of government, religion, and culture
3. Spanish word for town

Down
4. A huge sheet of moving ice
5. Movement from one place to another

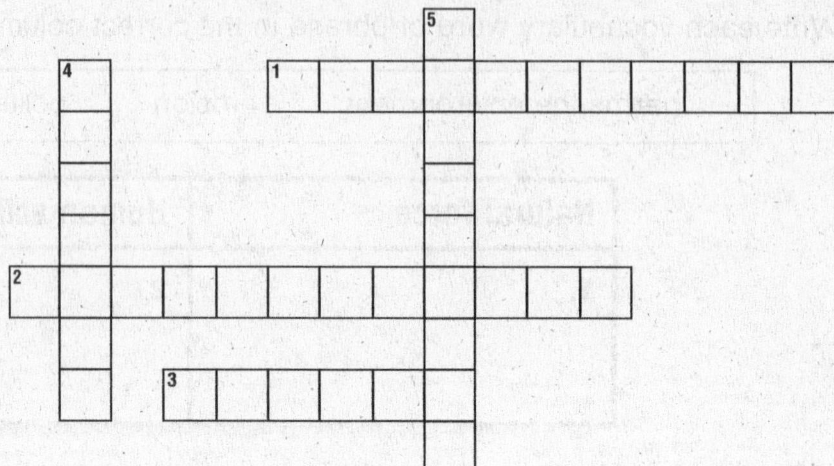

Study Guide

6. Read "People Arrive in the Americas." Then fill in the blanks below.

One theory about how the first _________________ came to the Americas is that they walked across a natural land bridge, which scientists named _________________. Beringia appeared between Alaska and _________________ during the _________________. Humans followed _________________ from Asia across Beringia into North America. These ancient Americans are known as _________________.

7. Read "Civilizations Develop." Then fill in the blanks below.

Over thousands of years, some Paleo-Indian groups _________________ large areas and built villages and cities. The Mound Builders built giant mounds where they often _________________. The Ancient Pueblo lived in the American _________________. Their buildings had many rooms. They also built underground rooms called _________________. The _________________ lived in central Mexico. They made their own calendar and built large _________________ to their gods.

Vocabulary and Study Guide

Vocabulary

Write the definition of each vocabulary word below.

1. surplus ____

2. potlatch ____

3. clan ____

4. Use two of the words in a sentence. _________________

____

____

Study Guide

Read "The Pacific Northwest." Then fill in the chart below.

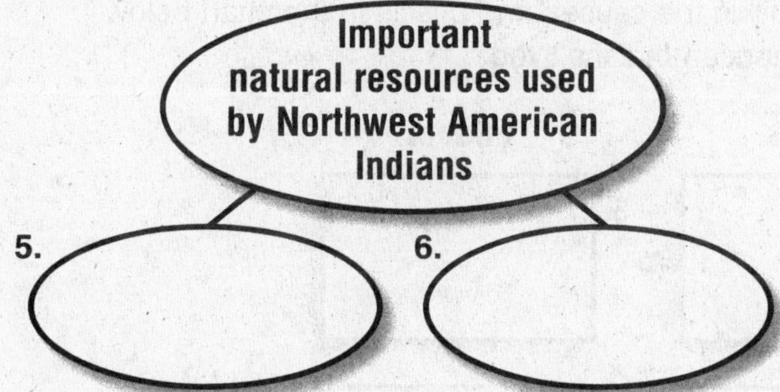

Read "The Tlingit." Then answer the questions below.

7. Out of what material did the Tlingit make their clothes? Why did they

use this material? _________________________________

____

____

8. What did the Tlingit do in the winter?

____

9. What Tlingit cultural traditions continue today? _____________

____

Vocabulary and Study Guide

Vocabulary

Write the definition of each vocabulary word below.

1. irrigation ____

____

2. staple ____

3. ceremony ____

____

4. Use two of the words in a sentence. _______________

____

Study Guide

Read "The Southwest." Then fill in the causes and effects in the chart below
to explain how Southwest American Indians lived.

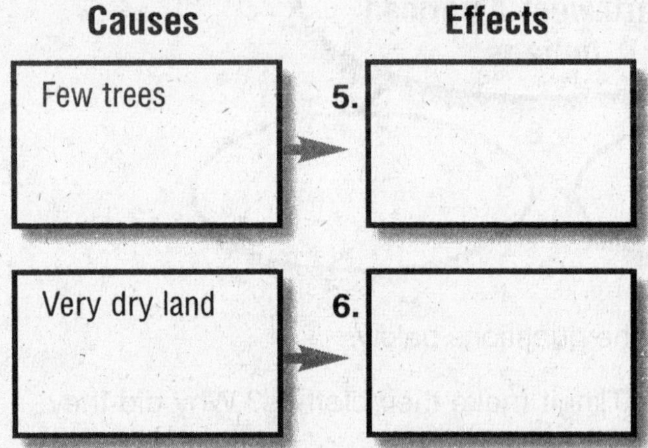

Read "The Hopi." Then choose the correct ending to each statement below.

7. At every meal, the Hopi ate

   A. beans.   **B.** corn.   **C.** squash.

8. Hopi religion said that they lived on the land to be

   A. farmers.   **B.** potters.   **C.** caretakers.

9. The Hopi used coal to make strong, hard

   A. adobe.   **B.** pottery.   **C.** irrigation pipes.

Vocabulary and Study Guide

Vocabulary

Write each vocabulary word in the correct column.

lodge	teepee	nomad	travois	farmer

Eastern Plains	Western Plains
1.	2.

Study Guide

Read "The Great Plains." Then answer the questions.

3. Why were Eastern Plains people able to farm more successfully than Western Plains people? _______________________________________

____

4. How did the Western Plains people use resources from buffalo to meet their needs? _______________________________________

____

____

Read "The Comanche." Then fill in the cause-and-effects chart below.

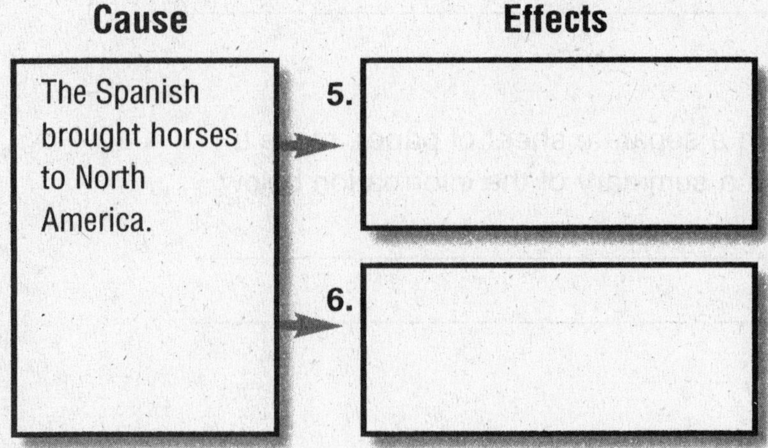

Skillbuilder: Summarize

Before agriculture, or farming, people lived by hunting animals and gathering plants. Around 9,000 years ago, some Paleo-Indians began to use agriculture to feed themselves. They gathered seeds of useful wild plants and learned to grow them as crops. People stopped migrating and began staying in one place to take care of their crops. A steady supply of food was available, and the population grew. Over time, the Paleo-Indians built large villages and cities.

Practice

Read the paragraph. Fill in the chart below. Then write a summary of the information.

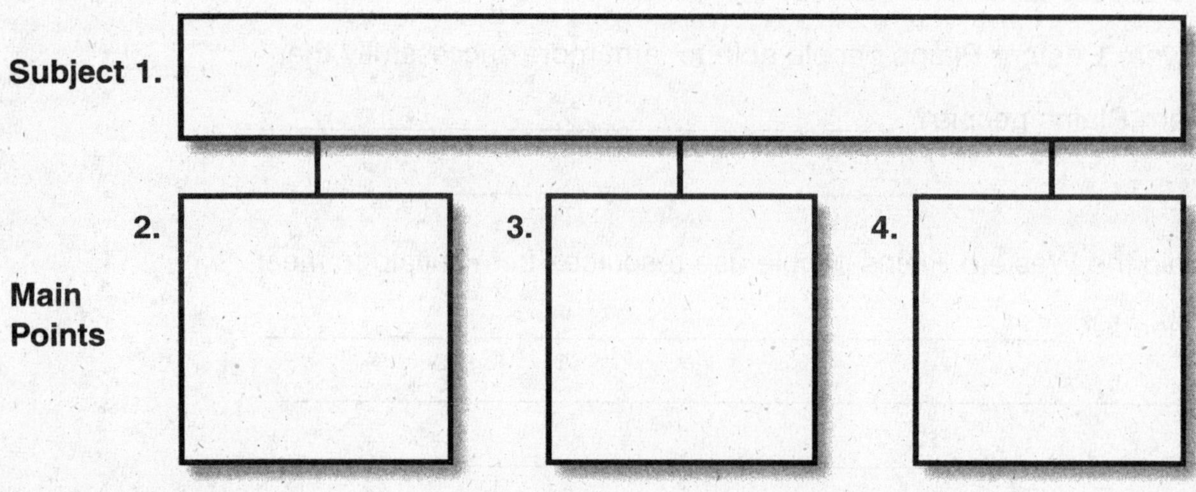

5. Summary: ____

____

Apply

Read "Tlingit Clans" in Lesson 2. On a separate sheet of paper, make a chart like the one above. Then write a summary of the information below.

Summary: ____

____

Vocabulary and Study Guide

Vocabulary

1. Draw a line connecting the vocabulary word to its meaning.

longhouse	A type of government in which groups join together
confederation	A symbol of an agreement used by Haudenosaunee
wampum	To exchange goods without using money
barter	A large shelter made of wooden poles and covered with bark

Study Guide

2. Read "The Eastern Woodlands." Then fill in the blanks below.

The Woodland people lived in a region that received a lot of

rain and had ample _____________________________. They got their

food by _____________________________ wild rice, hunting, and

farming. Most Woodland American Indians grew corn, squash, and

_____________________________. Farther north, the Haudenosaunee

built _____________________________ for shelter and wore

_____________________________ robes to protect them from the cold.

3. Read "The Haudenosaunee." Then fill in the blanks below.

Each Haudenosaunee clan was governed by a

_____________________________. These Haudenosaunee women

chose the _____________________________ for each group. The

chiefs from the Mohawk, Oneida, Onondaga, Cayuga, and

_____________________________ groups made up the governing

confederation of the _____________________________.

Almanac Map Practice

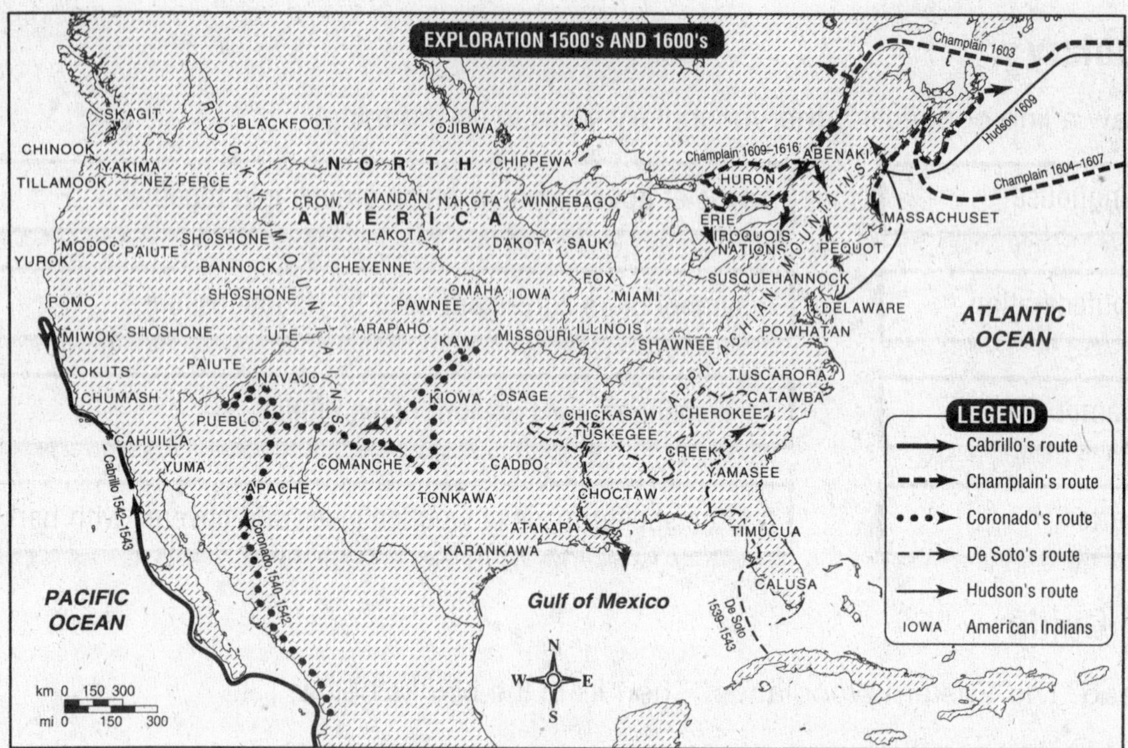

Use the map to do these activities and answer these questions.

Practice

1. Draw a line to trace Coronado's route.

2. What American Indian groups did Coronado likely meet? ___________

____

3. How many times did Champlain explore North America? In what years

   did these explorations take place? ___________________________

4. Circle the area covered by Cabrio's exploration.

5. Describe Hudson's journey using the directions *north*, *south*, *east*,

   and *west*. ____

Apply

6. Work with a partner to figure out the area where your state is on the
   map. Name any explorers who traveled through this area. Write the
   American Indian groups that lived in this area.

____

Almanac Graph Practice

Exploration in the 1500s

Exploration Today

Explorer	Distance	Time
de Soto	3,000 mi.	3 yrs.
Coronado	2,500 mi.	2 yrs.

Destination	Distance	Time
Moon	242,114 mi.	195 hrs.
Ocean Floor	4 mi.	3–4 hrs.

Practice

1. How many hours does it take for a rocket to travel from Earth to the

   Moon? ____

2. How many miles did Coronado travel on his trip? _________________

Apply

3. Read the paragraph. Then use the information below to complete the
   chart.

Different planets in the solar system have been explored using
unmanned probes. The probe named *Mariner 2* explored Venus in 1962.
Jupiter was explored by *Voyager 1* in 1977. Neptune was explored by
Voyager 2 in 1989. And the Mars Pathfinder landed on and explored
Mars in 1996.

Vocabulary and Study Guide

Vocabulary

Use each pair of words in a sentence.

1. merchant/China ____

____

2. caravan/salt ____

____

3. kingdom/trade ____

____

Study Guide

4. Read "Trade with China." Then fill in the blanks below.

Marco Polo was a _______________ from Italy who traveled

to _______________. There he saw inventions such as paper,

printing, and _______________. Many European merchants traveled

along the trade routes of the _______________ carrying silk and

spices back to Europe. Later, _______________ explorers sailed to

Africa in huge ships where they traded silk and _______________.

Read "African Trading Kingdoms." Then fill in the chart below.

Trading kingdom	Trade route	Cultural effect
Ghana	5.	7.
Mali	6.	8.

Name _______________________ Date __________

Vocabulary and Study Guide

Vocabulary

Write the definition of each vocabulary word below.

1. technology _______________________________________

2. navigation _______________________________________

3. astrolabe _______________________________________

____

4. profit _______________________________________

5. slavery _______________________________________

6. Use two words in a sentence.

____

Study Guide

Read "New Knowledge for Sailors." Then fill in the chart below.

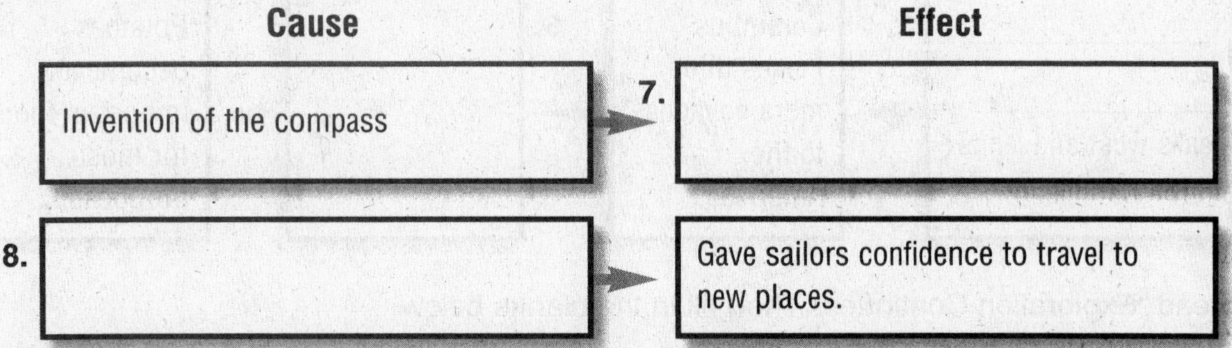

Read "A Sea Route to Asia." Then answer the questions.

9. What made Portugal a good starting place for sailors?

____

10. What did Bartolomeu Dias do to affect Portugal's trade routes?

____

____

11. Who led the first Portuguese voyage to India? _______________

Vocabulary and Study Guide

Vocabulary

Write the definition of each vocabulary word below.

1. settlement _______________________________

2. epidemic _______________________________

____

3. circumnavigate _______________________________

4. Use two of the words in a sentence.

____

____

Study Guide

Read "Christopher Columbus" and "The Columbian Exchange." Then fill in the sequence chart below.

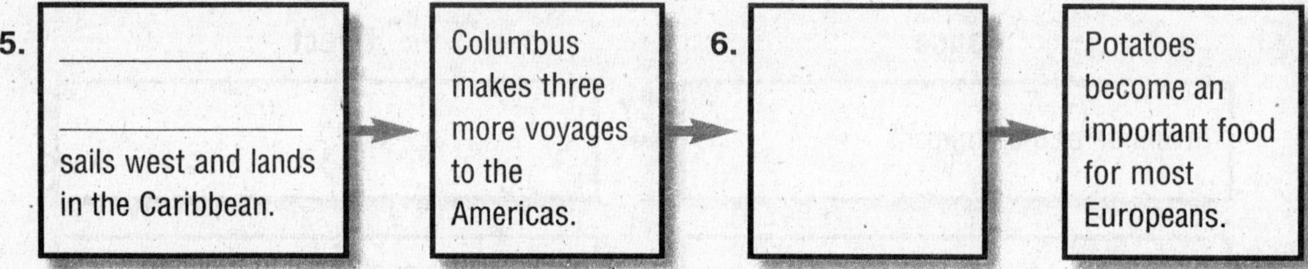

7. Read "Exploration Continues." Then fill in the blanks below.

_______________________ explored eastern South America

and claimed it for Portugal. _______________________, an Italian

explorer, made several voyages to South America and the Caribbean.

_______________________ sailed to present-day Panama in

Central America. Later, Ferdinand Magellan became the first

European to sail across the _______________________. Although

Magellan did not make it back to Spain, sailors from his crew did

successfully _______________________ the world.

Vocabulary and Study Guide

Vocabulary

Write each vocabulary word in the correct column.

conquistador	empire	expedition	person	thing	event

Aztec civilization	Francisco Pizzaro	Cortés's journey to Mexico
1.	2.	3.

Study Guide

Read "Cortés Conquers the Aztecs." Then answer the questions.

4. What were three things that helped Spain defeat the Aztecs?

____

____

____

5. What happened after Cortés conquered the Aztecs?

____

____

Read "Exploring North America." Then fill in the chart below.

Explorer	Goal	Achievement
Hernando de Soto	6.	7.
Francisco Vázquez de Coronado	8.	9.

Vocabulary and Study Guide

Vocabulary

Solve the clue and write the answer in the blank.
Then find the word in the puzzle. Look up, down,
forward, and backward.

1. A territory ruled by another country
   _____

2. A violent uprising against a ruler _____
3. A large farm or ranch _____
4. A community where priests taught
   Christianity _____
5. To change a religion or belief _____

A	N	T	L	O	V	E	R
D	Y	R	B	S	A	D	A
E	N	E	R	V	J	D	N
C	O	V	T	X	N	O	T
I	L	N	S	E	I	S	G
H	O	O	I	S	K	R	H
M	C	C	S	F	N	V	E
Q	A	I	G	E	P	A	M
H	M	T	U	I	R	W	I

Study Guide

6. Read "New Spain Grows."
   Then fill in the blanks below.

   After settling the colony of New Spain, explorers and

   _____________________ went north. They started missions

   where they worked to convert American Indians to

   _____________________ . Spanish settlers built forts called

   _____________________ to protect Spanish land claims.

   The Spanish were the first Europeans to settle the Southwest,

   Florida, and _____________________ .

7. Read "Life in New Spain." Then fill in the blanks below.

   The Spanish found good _____________________ in North

   America. They built _____________________ and forced American

   Indians to farm the land. Thousands of American Indians

   _____________________ from overwork. To replace these workers,

   Spain imported enslaved _____________________ .

   Some American Indians _____________________ to Catholicism,

   but others kept their own religions.

Skillbuilder: Use Latitude and Longitude

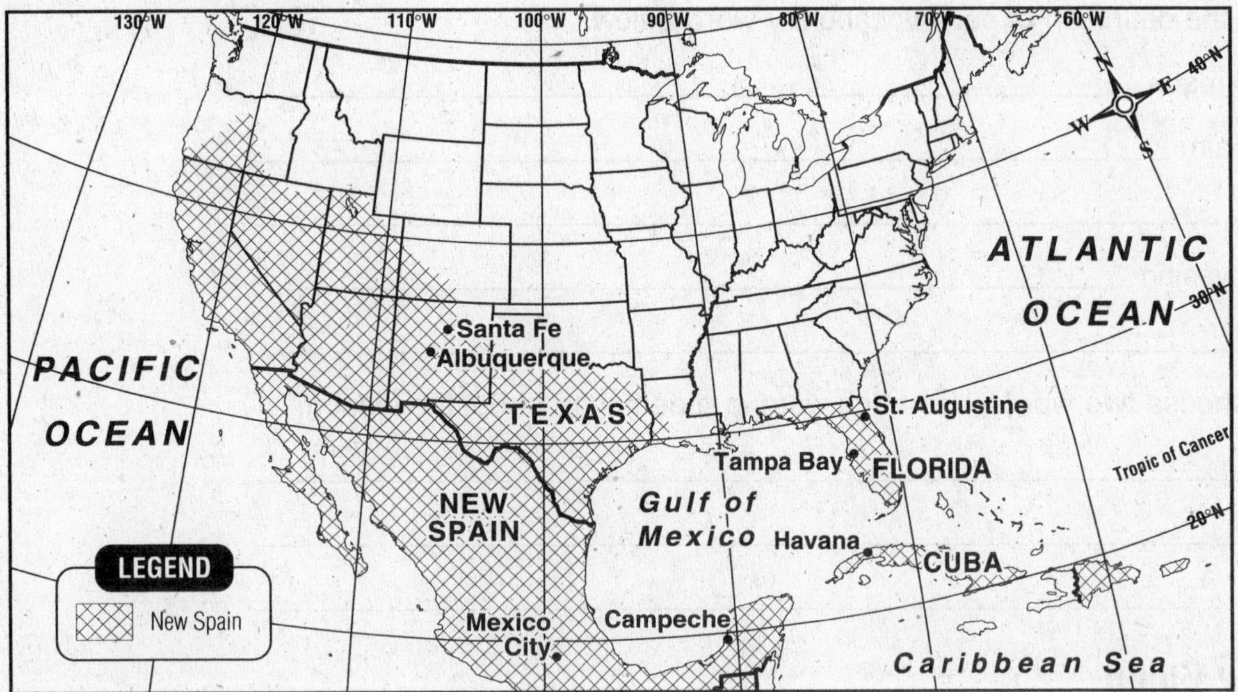

Practice

1. On what line of latitude is St. Augustine located? _________________

2. What lines of latitude and longitude are closest to Mexico City?

____

3. About how many degrees of longitude are there between Mexico City

and the city of Campeche? _________________________

4. What state covers the point at 30° north latitude and 100° west

longitude? _________________________

Apply

Is the area of the world shown in the map to the north or to the south of
the equator? How do you know?

____

____

   21   Use with *United States History*, pp. 116–117

Vocabulary and Study Guide

Vocabulary

Write the definition of each vocabulary word below.

1. armada _________________________________

2. claim _________________________________

____

3. invasion _________________________________

____

4. Choose two words. Use each word in a sentence about the lesson.

____

____

____

Study Guide

Read "Searching for a Passage to Asia." Then fill in the chart below.

Explorer	Explored North America for this nation	What this explorer did
John Cabot	**5.**	**6.**
Giovanni da Verrazano	**7.**	**8.**
9.	**10.**	Founded Quebec
Henry Hudson	**11.** The Netherlands and ____________	**12.** ____________ and found the body of water now called the Hudson Bay

Skillbuilder: Use Parallel Timelines

Dutch

Swedish

Practice

1. Which one of the two groups first set up a colony in the Americas?

____

2. Which colony became English around 1660?

____

3. Describe how the settlements changed.

____

____

____

Apply

Read about the French explorers in Lesson 4. Note the dates of the different explorers. Then list important events on the two timelines. Use one timeline for LaSalle and one for Marquette and Jolliet.

Vocabulary and Study Guide

Vocabulary

Solve the clue and write the answer in the blank.
Then find the word in the puzzle. Look up, down,
forward, and backward.

1.	A crop that people grow and sell to earn money
2.	A piece of ownership of a company
3.	To put money into something to try to make more money
4.	A document that gives certain freedoms to a person or group

A	I	X	D	K	G	S	C
M	S	V	F	D	G	T	N
C	A	S	H	C	R	O	P
H	P	B	L	T	N	C	D
A	R	M	E	U	Y	K	Q
R	E	Q	O	K	O	I	J
T	H	I	N	V	E	S	T
E	S	Z	R	C	T	A	C
R	H	U	W	L	F	J	B

Study Guide

5. Read "The Lost Colony." Then fill in the blanks below.

In 1585, about 100 men from England settled on

_________________. Most of them returned to _________________

because they could not grow crops. In 1587, the English tried again to

settle there. When _________________ returned from a trip to England

to get more supplies, the _________________ had disappeared.

6. Read "The Jamestown Colony." Then fill in the blanks below.

A group of English merchants started the

_________________ in 1606. They wanted to build

a _________________ in North America. The

company sent men and boys there to build a fort. The settlers named

their colony _________________.

Vocabulary and Study Guide

Vocabulary

1. Draw a line connecting the vocabulary word to its meaning.

compact	A strip of land that stretches into a body of water
pilgrim	An agreement
cape	A person who makes a long journey for religious reasons

Study Guide

Read "The Plymouth Colony" and "Massachusetts Bay Colony." Then fill in the chart below to compare the colonies.

	Plymouth Colony	Massachusetts Bay Colony
Who settled there?	2.	3.
Why did they settle there?	4.	5.
What year did they settle there?	6.	7.

Name _________________________________ Date _____________

Vocabulary and Study Guide

Vocabulary

When you add a suffix to the end of a base word, you make a new word. Knowing a suffix and its base word can help you understand unfamiliar words. Look at the word *ability*.

Able	-ity	Ability
"having the skill to do something"	"the state of being"	"the state of being able"

Break down the vocabulary word into its base word and suffix. Write its meaning.

-ity "the state of being"

-ary "a person who does something"

1. diverse = diverse + -ity

Diversity means _________________________________

____

2. missionary = _______________ + _______________

Missionary means _________________________________

____

Study Guide

3. Read "New Netherland." Then fill in the outline below.

   I. Main Idea: _________________________________

____

     A. Supporting Idea: _________________________________

____

       1. Detail: _________________________________

____

       2. Detail: _________________________________

____

Almanac Map Practice

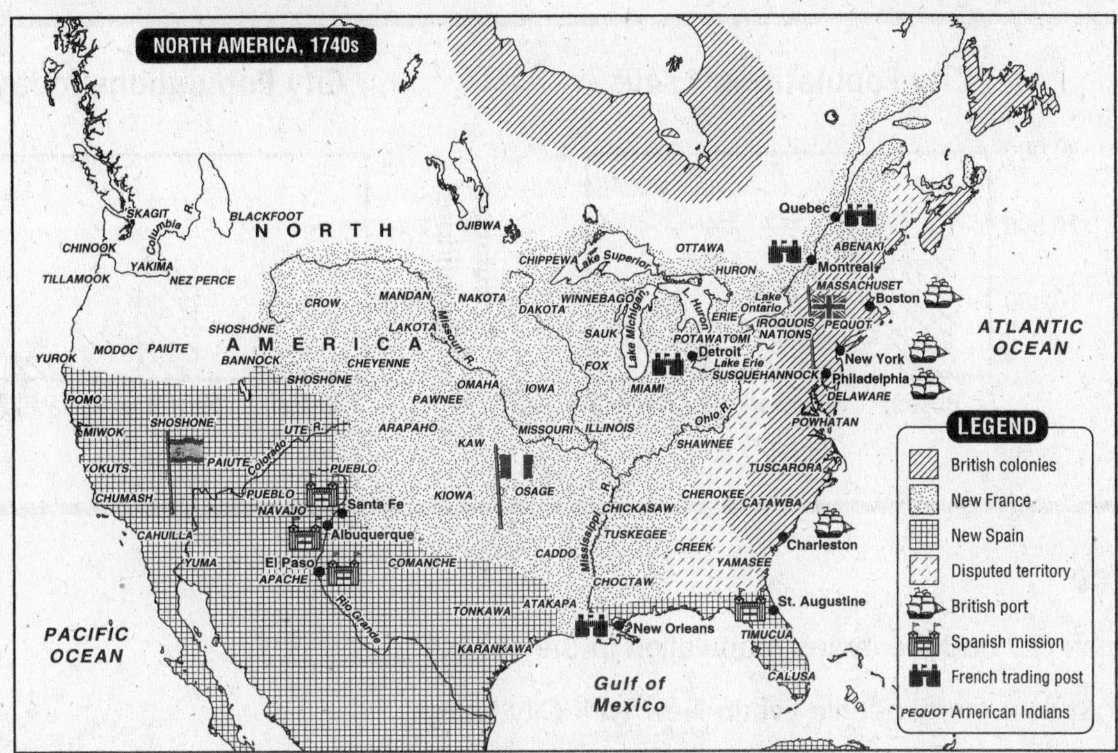

Use the map to do these activities and answer these questions.

Practice

1. Draw a box around Spanish missions along the Rio Grande.

2. Draw a triangle around the French trading post that is the farthest north in New France.

3. What is the name of this trading post? _______________________

4. Draw a circle around the area of the Disputed Territory.

5. Which American Indians lived in this area? _______________

____

Apply

6. Work with a partner. Read about New York City and Philadelphia in "City Life" in Lesson 2 of Chapter 6.

   Look at the map. Why do you think that New York City and Philadelphia were centers of trade?

____

Almanac Graph Practice

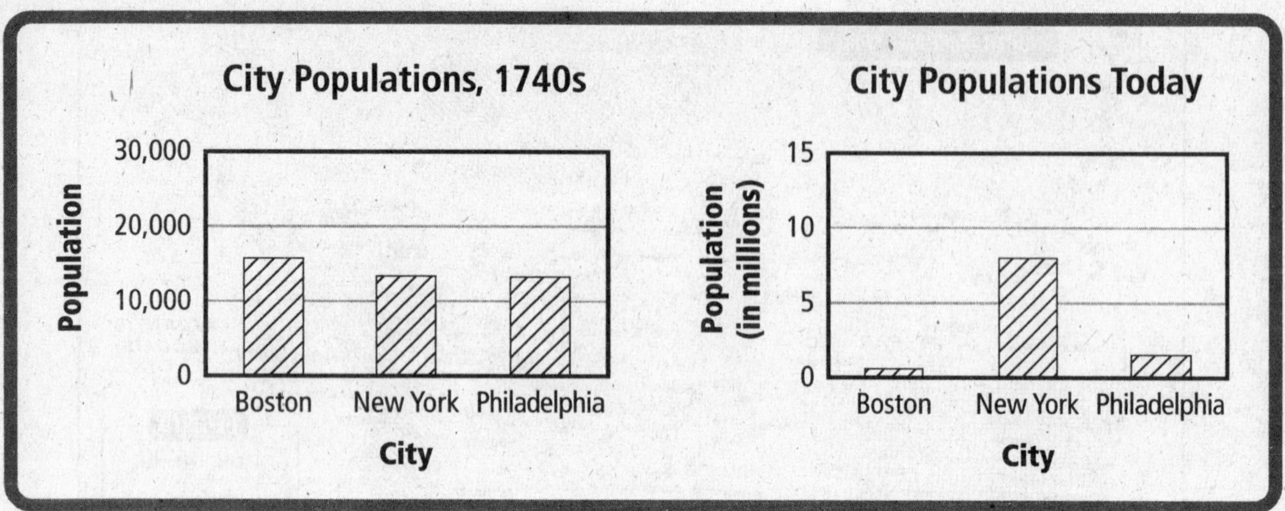

Practice

1. Which city had the largest population in the 1740s? ________________

2. About how many people live in New York City today?

____

Apply

3. Use the information in the chart below to make a bar graph of the population of Baltimore.

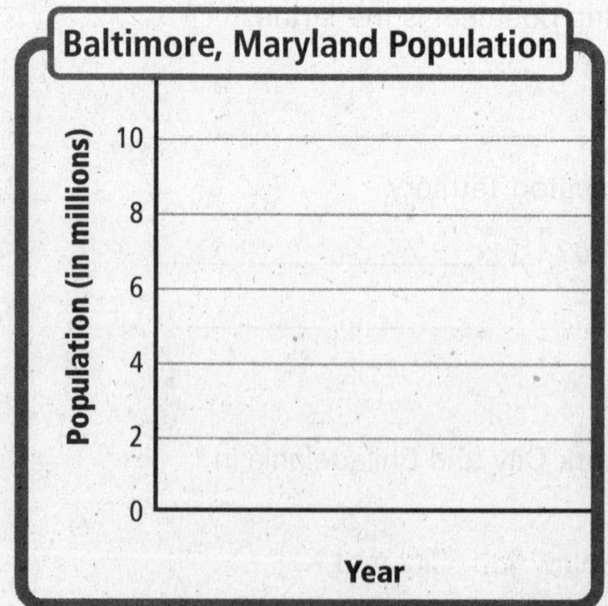

Baltimore, Maryland Population

Year	Population
1920	733,826
1960	939,024
2000	651,154

Use with *United States History*, pp. 156–157

Vocabulary and Study Guide

Vocabulary

If you do not know a word's meaning, try breaking it into smaller parts.
It may contain a smaller word that you know.

Find the smaller words inside these words. Use what you know about the
smaller word or words to write the meaning of the longer word.

	New word	Words in it that I know	Word meanings that I know	What I think the word means
1.	fall line			
2.	growing season			
3.	tidewater			
4.	backcountry			

Study Guide

Read "Geography of the Colonies." Then fill in the compare and contrast chart
below.

	Land	Climate/growing season	Natural resources
New England	Mountains and deep valleys; Rocky, sandy soil	5.	6.
Middle Colonies	7.	8.	9.
Southern Colonies	10.	11.	12.

Vocabulary and Study Guide

Vocabulary

Write the definition of each vocabulary word below.

1. dissenter ____

____

2. banish ____

3. town meeting ____

____

4. self-government ____

____

Study Guide

Read "Massachusetts." Then fill in the sequence chart below.

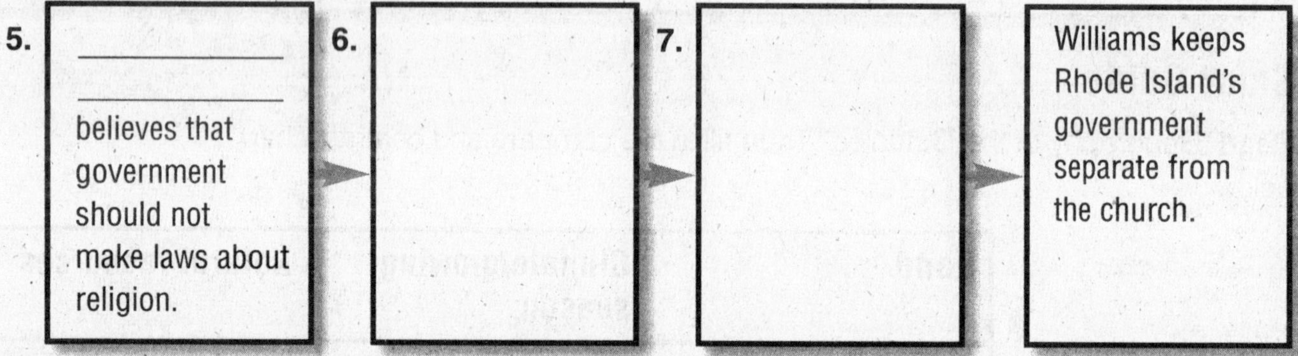

Read "Conflicts over Land." Then choose the correct ending to each statement below.

8. Colonists and American Indians had conflicts because of different views about

  A. farming.   **B.** land ownership.   **C.** war.

9. The Pequot War ended when most of the Pequot Indians had been

  A. killed.   **B.** forced to leave.   **C.** enslaved.

10. The war between the colonists and the Wampanoag was called

  A. Metacomet's War.   **B.** the New England War.   **C.** King Philip's War.

Vocabulary and Study Guide

Vocabulary

Across
1. A good brought into one country from another
2. Part of the triangular trade route from Africa to the West Indies
3. The business of buying and selling human beings

Down
1. All the businesses that make one type of product
2. Traders bought enslaved people from this continent
3. Ships from Europe carried spices, goods, and _____
4. A product sent to another country and sold

Study Guide

7. Read "Using the Sea." Then fill in the blanks below.

   The geography of New England made the success of the

   _______________ , _______________ , and _______________

   industries possible. New England merchants exported fish and

   lumber as part of the _______________ route between North

   America, Europe, and _______________ .

8. Read "Home and Community Life." Then fill in the blanks below.

   New England families often had _______________ or

   _______________ children and lived in a house with

   _______________ main room. A _______________ and

   sleeping mattresses might be the only furniture. Puritan families

   wanted everyone to be able to read the _______________ .

   Massachusetts passed a law that said that towns with more than

   50 people had to build a _______________ .

Skillbuilder: Make a Line Graph

Massachusetts Colony, 1680–1730

Year	Estimated Population (in thousands)
1680	39.8
1690	49.5
1700	55.9
1710	62.4
1720	91.0
1730	114.1

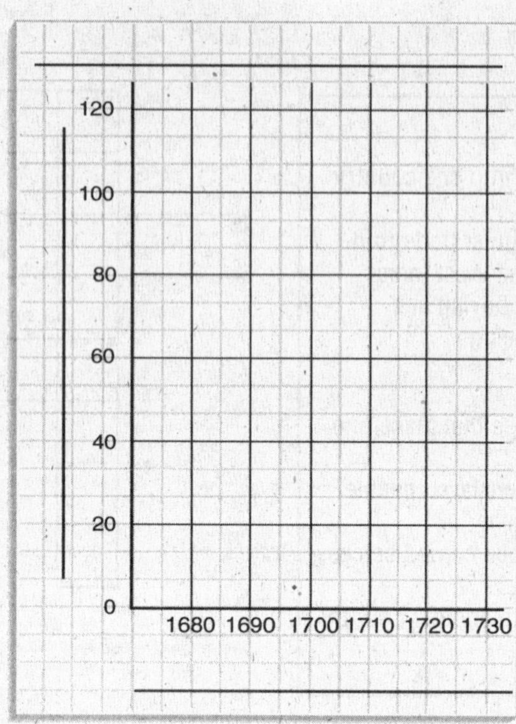

Practice

1. Label the horizontal axis on the graph.

2. Label the vertical axis on the graph.

3. Draw dots on the graph to show the data in the table. Then draw a line to connect the dots.

4. Give the graph a title.

Apply the Skill

Use your graph skills to draw your own line graph. Research and collect data that shows how the area where you live has changed over time. You can go to the library or call your town or county government. Arrange the data in a table, and then show it on a line graph. Draw your line graph on a separate sheet of paper.

Practice Book

Use with *United States History*, pp. 182–183

Vocabulary and Study Guide

Vocabulary

1. proprietor _______________________________________

____

2. representative ___________________________________

____

3. treaty ____

4. Use two of the words in a sentence.

____

____

Study Guide

Read "New York and New Jersey." Then fill in the chart below to show how government worked in the colonies of New York and New Jersey.

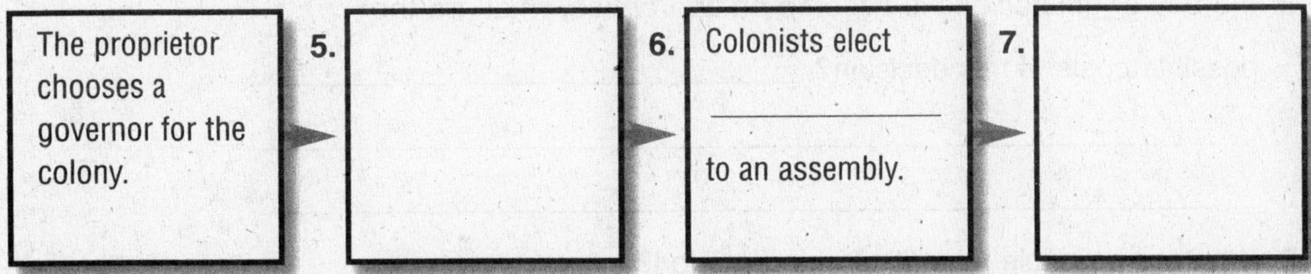

Read "Pennsylvania and Delaware." Then fill in the chart below with each person's contribution to the Middle Colonies.

William Penn	Benjamin Franklin
8.	9.

CHAPTER 6

Skillbuilder: Make a Decision

Many young people who lived in towns and cities became apprentices. An apprentice is someone who studies with a master to learn a skill or business. As a child, an apprentice often lived in the master's house. Apprentices usually worked with their masters for four to seven years. Boy apprentices learned shoemaking, printing, bookmaking, and other skills. Girl apprentices learned how to spin thread and weave cloth. By watching and helping, apprentices gained the skills they needed to enter the business as adults.

Practice

1. From reading the passage, what is an apprentice? _______________

   ____

   ____

2. If a boy or girl decides to become an apprentice, what are the

   possible costs of this decision? ________________________________

   ____

   ____

3. What are possible benefits of this decision? ______________________

   ____

   ____

Apply

Read about William Penn in "Pennsylvania and Delaware" in Lesson 1. Penn made many important decisions when he founded Pennsylvania. Choose one of his decisions and write the benefits and costs of it. What might have happened if Penn had made a different decision? Write a paragraph explaining how Penn might have acted differently.

 34 **Use with *United States History*, pp. 194–195**

Vocabulary and Study Guide

Vocabulary

Write the definition of each vocabulary word below.

1. free enterprise ____

2. free market economy ____

3. artisan ____

4. laborer ____

5. apprentice ____

6. Use two words in a sentence.

____

____

Study Guide

Read "A Mix of People." Then answer the questions.

7. Why did the Middle Colonies have a diverse population?

____

____

Read "Making a Living." Then fill in the chart below.

Workers in the country	Workers in the city
8.	9.

Vocabulary and Study Guide

Vocabulary

Following the example below, break down the vocabulary word into its root and suffix. Then write its meaning.

> -tion "the state of" or "the result of"
> -ure "a group with a specific function"
> -or "one who does a certain thing"

Example:

> **Conductor =** conduct "to lead or to guide" + -or
> Conductor means "one who leads or guides."

1. plantation = ___________________________ + ___________________________

Plantation means ____

2. legislature = ___________________________ + ___________________________

Legislature means ____

3. debtor = ___________________________ + ___________________________

Debtor means ____

Study Guide

Read "New Colonies in the South." Then fill in the chart below.

Colony	Maryland	Carolinas	Georgia
Why it was founded	4.	5.	6.

Vocabulary and Study Guide

Vocabulary

Solve the clue and write the answer in the blank. Then find the word in the puzzle. Look up, down, forward, and backward. Look for a bonus word!

1. An African American religious folk song _______

2. A plant used to color clothing blue _______

3. An area where rivers rise and fall with ocean tides _______

4. A person who directs the work of other people _______

Bonus Word: _______

A	D	T	H	L	Z	S	H
R	F	I	I	A	R	O	A
C	E	D	L	U	P	G	U
B	J	E	M	T	B	I	G
A	V	W	S	I	D	D	E
N	I	A	P	R	J	N	R
J	K	T	Q	I	E	I	L
O	Y	E	T	P	M	V	F
X	R	R	W	S	U	E	O

Study Guide

5. Read "Southern Agriculture" and "Plantations and Small Farms." Then fill in the blanks below.

The main cash crops in the South were tobacco, ________________, and ________________. Although the South is known for its plantations, most southern colonists lived on ________________ in the backcountry. Children on plantations learned to read and write from ________________. In the backcountry, children only learned to read or write if their ________________ could teach them.

6. Read "Southern Slavery." Then fill in the blanks below.

As the number of ________________ grew, more enslaved Africans were brought to North America. Planters ________________ enslaved Africans as property and forced them to work in the ________________ or as ________________. To survive their hardships, enslaved Africans created close ________________ and religious ________________.

Almanac Map Practice

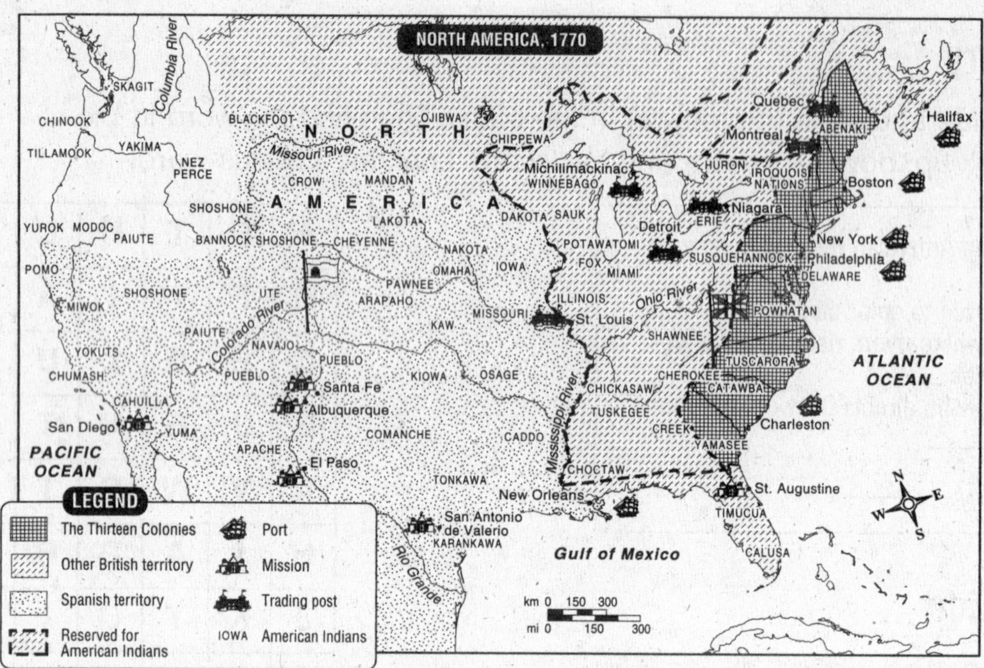

Use the map to do these activities and answer these questions.

Practice

1. Along which river did the Lakota live? ___________________

2. Draw a box around the trading post that is farthest north.

3. About how many miles is it from the mission at Santa Fe to the mission at El Paso? ___________________

4. Color in the Massachusetts colony.

5. Circle all of the ports along the Atlantic coast that were used by the British.

6. Which trading post is the farthest west? ___________________

Apply

7. With a partner, study the map "North America in 1750" in Chapter 7, Lesson 1. Compare this map to the one on the top of this page. Did the same nation control the land just west of the Mississippi River from 1750 to 1770? How can you tell?

____

____

Almanac Graph Practice

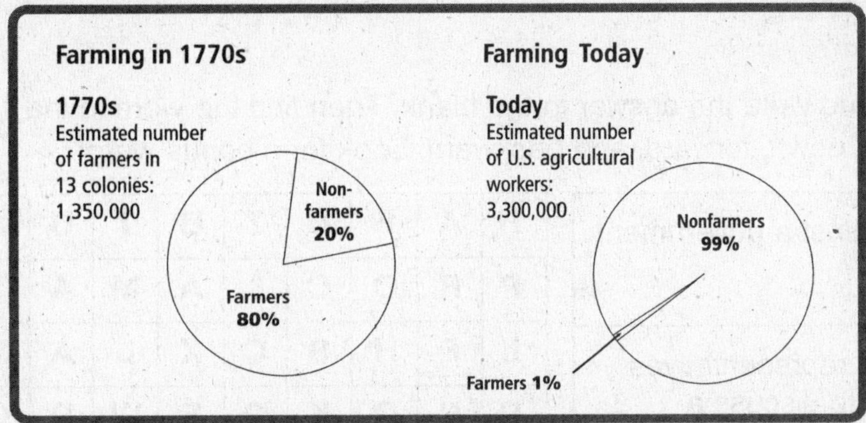

Practice

1. Were there more nonfarmers in the 1770s or today? _______________

2. About how many people worked on farms in the 1770s?

____

Apply

3. Use the information below to complete the circle graphs. Draw lines to make sections in each circle. Write the term *employed* or *unemployed* in each section.

> In 1982, 9.7% of American workers were unemployed, or did not have jobs. This was far higher than in 1944, when only 1.2% of American workers were unemployed.

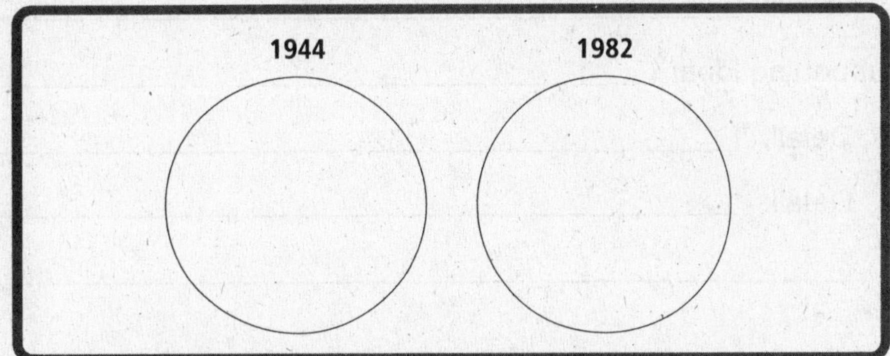

Vocabulary and Study Guide

Vocabulary

Solve the clue and write the answer in the blank. Then find the word in the puzzle. Look up, down, forward, and backward. Look for a bonus word!

1.	A fight against a government
2.	A group of representatives who meet to discuss a subject
3.	An official public statement
4.	A person or group that joins with another to work toward a goal
	Bonus Word:

H	A	F	D	Z	B	T	U	J	W	G	M
P	R	O	C	L	A	M	A	T	I	O	N
L	E	H	S	C	X	L	A	M	W	V	U
B	B	O	K	O	E	W	P	Q	C	E	O
F	E	V	Y	N	C	A	K	J	H	R	L
A	L	L	Y	G	T	D	L	N	S	N	P
R	L	I	N	R	N	E	M	K	G	M	S
O	I	B	U	E	F	O	X	P	D	E	R
G	O	J	Z	S	R	Q	P	Y	I	N	B
A	N	C	M	S	P	E	G	I	K	T	F

Study Guide

5. Read "War Between France and Britain." Then fill in the outline below.

I. Main Idea: ____

____

A. Supporting Idea: ___________________________________

1. Detail: _________________________________

2. Detail: _________________________________

B. Supporting Idea: ___________________________________

1. Detail: _________________________________

2. Detail: _________________________________

____

Vocabulary and Study Guide

Vocabulary

Write the definition of each vocabulary word below.

1. boycott ____

2. tax ____
   ____

3. protest ____
   ____

4. repeal ____

5. liberty ____
   ____

6. smuggling ____

7. Choose two words. Use each word in a sentence about the lesson.

   ____

   ____

Study Guide

Read "Early Conflicts with Britain." Then fill in the comparison chart below.

What the British government wanted	What the colonists wanted
8.	9.

Vocabulary and Study Guide

Vocabulary

1. Draw a line connecting the vocabulary word to its meaning.

correspondence	To provide people with food and shelter
massacre	Someone chosen to speak and act for others
delegate	The killing of many people
quarter	Written communication

Study Guide

2. Read "Trouble in Boston." Then fill in the blanks below.

The people of ________________________________ were

angry with the British government. The colonists did not want

________________________________ in their city. A fight started

on ________________________, 1770.

________________________________, an African American

sailor, was killed in the fight. This event came to be known as

the ________________________________. When the British

soldiers were put on trial, ________________________________

defended them. In 1772, Samuel Adams set up

________________________________ to help colonists

share news about the British.

Name ___________________________ Date ___________

Skillbuilder: Identify Causes and Effects

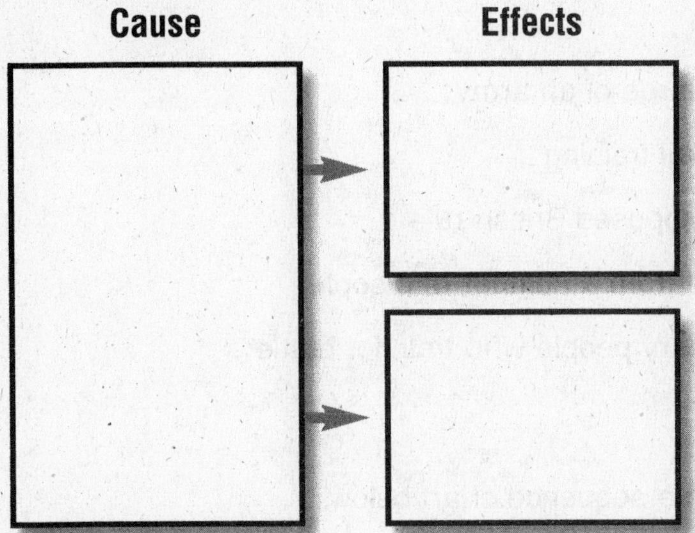

Practice

1. What is the first effect of Britain needing money? ___________________

2. What is the second effect of Britain needing money?

____

3. Why are the Stamp Act and Townshend Acts effects of Britain needing money?

____

____

Apply

Now you can use your cause and effect skills to show another version of events. Many times an effect can cause another event or action. Read "The Boston Tea Party." Fill in the chart with the cause and effect of the Boston Tea Party.

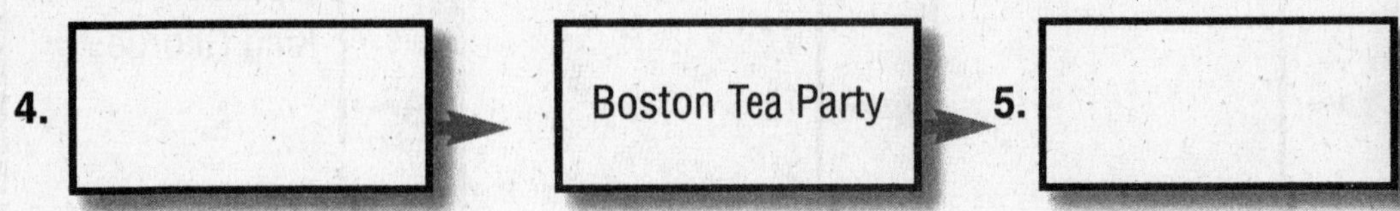

Vocabulary and Study Guide

Vocabulary

Write the word for each definition below.

1. _________________ The officer in charge of an army

2. _________________ Militia with special training

3. _________________ A colonist who opposed British rule

4. _________________ A written request from a number of people

5. _________________ A group of ordinary people who train for battle

Study Guide

Read "Moving Toward War." Then fill in the sequence chart below.

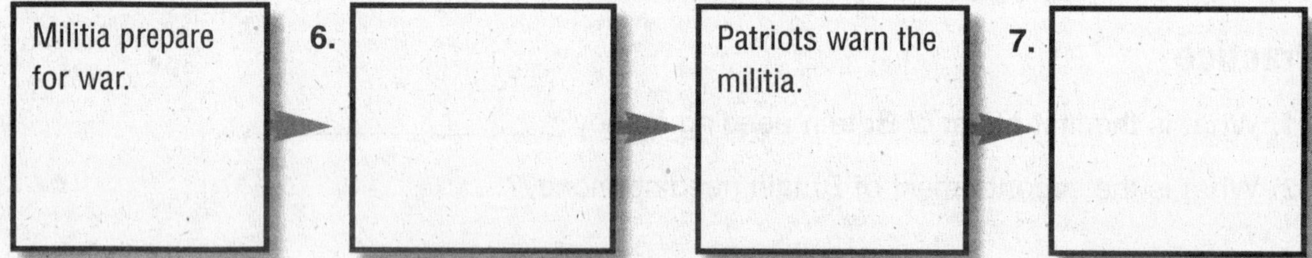

Read "The First Battles." Then fill in the sequence chart below.

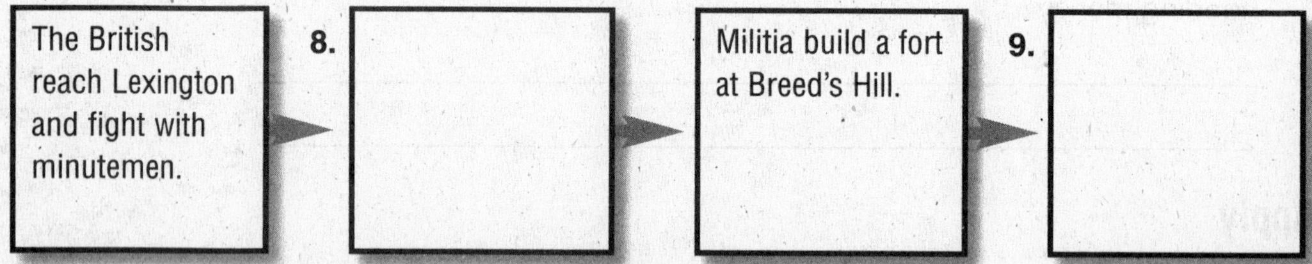

Read "A Colonial Army." Then fill in the sequence chart below.

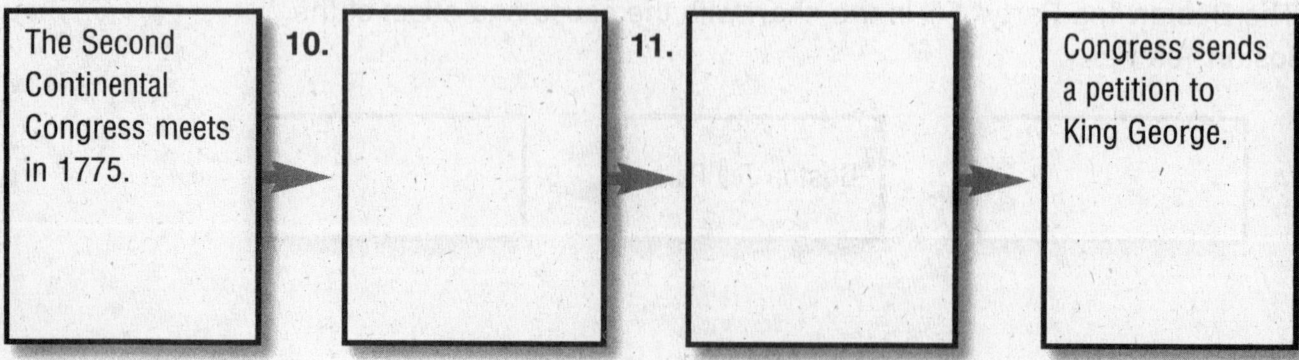

Vocabulary and Study Guide

Vocabulary

Across

1. A statement that announces an idea
2. Freedom from being ruled by someone else

Down

3. Freedoms protected by law
4. The crime of fighting against one's own government

Study Guide

5. Read "The Steps to Independence." Then fill in the blanks below.

Thomas Paine wrote a small, inexpensive booklet called

________________________. In the booklet, he explained that

________________________ treated the ________________________

unfairly. He said the only way to stop this unfair treatment was for the

colonies to become ________________________. After reading Paine's

booklet, many people who had ________________________ to

separate from Britain changed their minds.

6. Read "Declaration of Independence." Then fill in the blanks below.

Among the readers of Paine's booklet were the delegates of the

________________________. This group asked five delegates, including

________________________ to write a ________________________ to

tell other countries and colonists why a break with Britain was needed.

Jefferson said that people have certain ________________________

that no one can take away. The delegates signed the document on

________________________.

Vocabulary and Study Guide

Vocabulary

Write the definition of each vocabulary word below.

1. neutral ____

2. inflation ____

3. Loyalist ____

4. Use two words in a sentence.

____

____

Study Guide

5. Read "Life During the War." Then draw a line connecting each person to what that person did.

Joseph Brant	Stayed at camp to help the soldiers
Peter Salem	Dressed in men's clothes and joined the American army
Deborah Sampson	Urged the Mohawk people to side with the British
Martha Washington	Fought in the Battle of Bunker Hill after being freed
Mary Ludwig Hays	Fought in her husband's place

Vocabulary and Study Guide

Vocabulary

As you read the chapter, fill in the word webs.

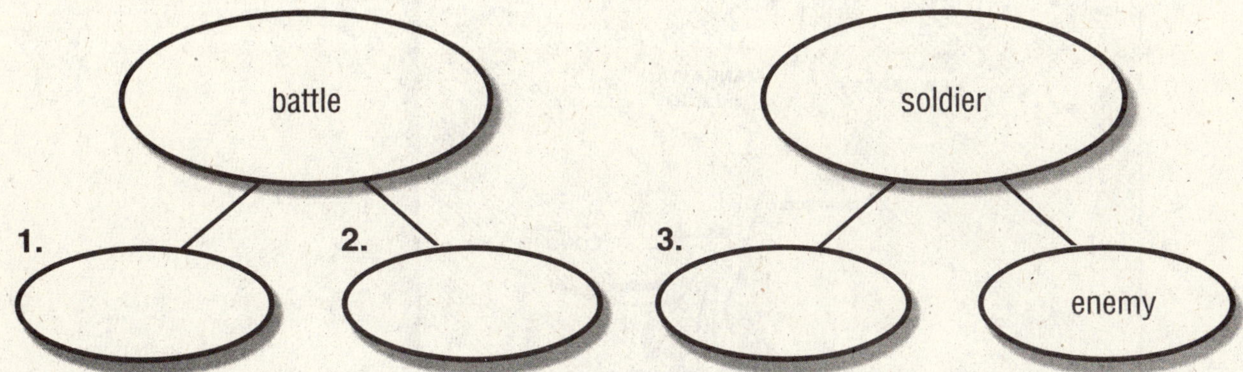

Study Guide

Read "Washington's First Battles." Then fill in the sequence chart below.

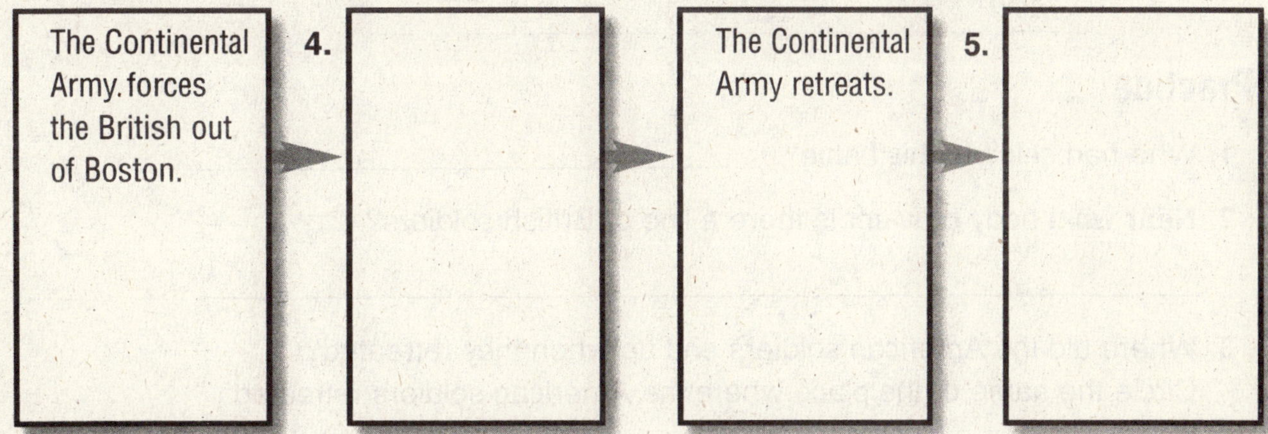

Read "A Turning Point." Then fill in the sequence chart below.

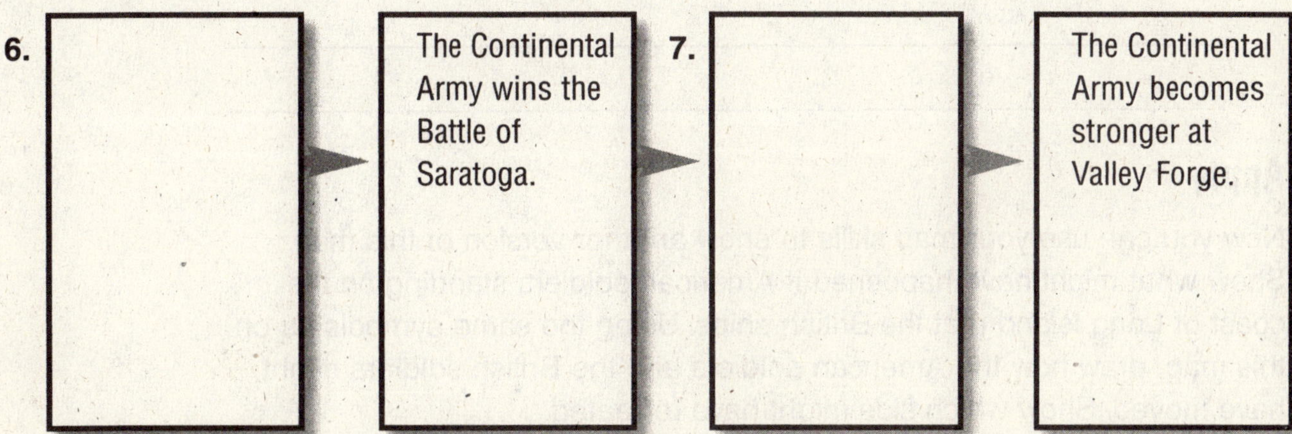

Skillbuilder: Read a Battle Map

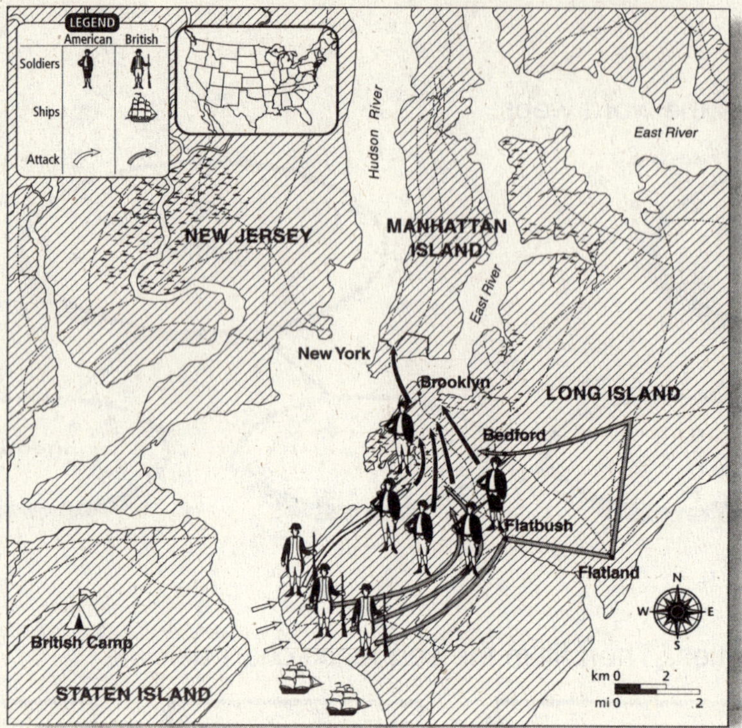

Practice

1. Who had ships in this battle? ________________________________

2. Near what body of water is there a line of British soldiers?

____

3. Where did the American soldiers end up when they retreated?
Circle the name of the place where the American soldiers retreated.

4. Did all of the British soldiers attack by moving in the same direction?
What direction or directions did they travel? ________________

____

____

Apply

Now you can use your map skills to show another version of this map.
Show what might have happened if American soldiers standing on the
coast of Long Island met the British ships. Using the same symbols as on
this map, draw how the American soldiers and the British soldiers might
have moved. Show which side might have retreated.

   48   Use with *United States History*, pp. 284–285

Vocabulary and Study Guide

Vocabulary

1. Draw a line connecting the vocabulary word to its meaning.

traitor	Someone who is not loyal
surrender	A plan of action
strategy	To give up

Study Guide

Read "Winning the War." Then fill in the compare and contrast chart below.

	What did the British do?	**What did the Americans do?**
The war in the South	2.	3.
The war in the West	Lost the war in the West	Won the war in the West
The Battle of Yorktown	4.	5.

Vocabulary and Study Guide

Vocabulary

Write the definition of each vocabulary word below.

1. territory   _______________________________

____

2. constitution   _______________________________

3. ordinance   _______________________________

4. citizen   _______________________________

5. Use two of the words in a sentence.

____

____

Study Guide

Read "The Articles of Confederation." Then fill in the cause and effects chart below.

Cause   **Effects**

Cause	Effects
The Articles of Confederation	Created a national government
	Could not make the states work together
	6.
	7.
	8.

Vocabulary and Study Guide

Vocabulary

Solve the clue and write the answer in the blank. Then find the word in the
puzzle. Look up, down, forward, and backward. Look for a bonus word!

1.	An agreement reached in which each side gives up something that it wants
2.	A government in which the citizens elect leaders to represent them
3.	A system in which the states share power with the central government
4.	To accept or officially approve
Bonus Word:	

C	O	X	B	C	N	R	M	E	A
W	J	S	K	O	L	T	I	H	U
V	X	L	D	M	Y	I	E	R	W
A	Q	R	E	P	U	B	L	I	C
F	E	D	E	R	A	L	S	P	E
A	K	G	F	O	F	Z	T	G	C
S	C	H	P	M	H	B	U	D	Q
M	R	A	T	I	F	Y	J	N	G
D	M	Y	K	S	L	V	O	I	J
N	F	R	E	E	D	O	M	Z	B

Study Guide

5. Read "Leaders of the Convention." Then fill in the blanks below.

Fifty-five delegates met in Philadelphia in 1787 for the

__________________________. They wanted to create a

__________________________, or a government in which citizens

elect leaders. One delegate, James Madison, had a plan for a new

system of government. Other important delegates were

__________________________ and __________________________.

6. Read "Creating a New Government." Then fill in the blanks below.

The delegates wanted a federal system that allows states to share

power. The __________________________ divided Congress into

two parts, the Senate and the __________________________.

After the delegates made decisions, they had to

__________________________ the Constitution.

Skillbuilder: Understand Point of View

> "I have no fear but that the result of our experiment [new government] will be that men may be trusted to govern themselves without a master."
>
> —Thomas Jefferson
>
> "It has been observed that a pure democracy, it if were practicable [attainable], would be the most perfect government. Experience has proved that no position [opinion] is more false than this."
>
> —Alexander Hamilton

Practice

1. From reading the chapter, what do you already know about Alexander Hamilton's experience and beliefs? _______________________________

   ____

2. What was Alexander Hamilton's point of view? _______________________

   ____

3. What was Thomas Jefferson's point of view? _______________________

   ____

4. Explain how knowing these two points of view can help you understand why Jefferson was against the national bank and why

   Hamilton was for the national bank. _______________________________

   ____

   ____

Apply

What experiences and beliefs affect your own point of view about the powers of the federal government? On a separate sheet of paper, write a paragraph expressing your point of view about government.

Vocabulary and Study Guide

Vocabulary

Across

1. Checks and _______
2. Laws that do not agree with the Constitution are _______ .
3. A government in which the people have the power to make political decisions

Down

4. A change to the Constitution
5. To reject a law

Study Guide

6. Read "Changing the Constitution." Then fill in the outline below.

  I. Main Idea: ___________________________________

         ____

    A. A change can be made with an amendment.

      1. Detail: _______________________________

           ____

           ____

      2. Detail: Three-fourths of the states must also ratify it.

    B. The Bill of Rights is a list of amendments written in 1791.

      1. Detail: _______________________________

           ____

           ____

      2. Detail: _______________________________

           ____

           ____

Practice Book

Use with *United States History*, pp. 312–317

Vocabulary and Study Guide

Vocabulary

Write the vocabulary word that matches each definition.

1. A group chosen by the President to help run the executive branch

   ____

2. The city where the government meets _______________

3. A group of people who share similar ideas about government

   ____

4. The official ceremony to make someone President

   ____

5. What people pay to borrow money _______________

6. Use two of the vocabulary words in a sentence.

   ____

   ____

Study Guide

Read "Arguments in the Cabinet." Then fill in the Venn diagram below.

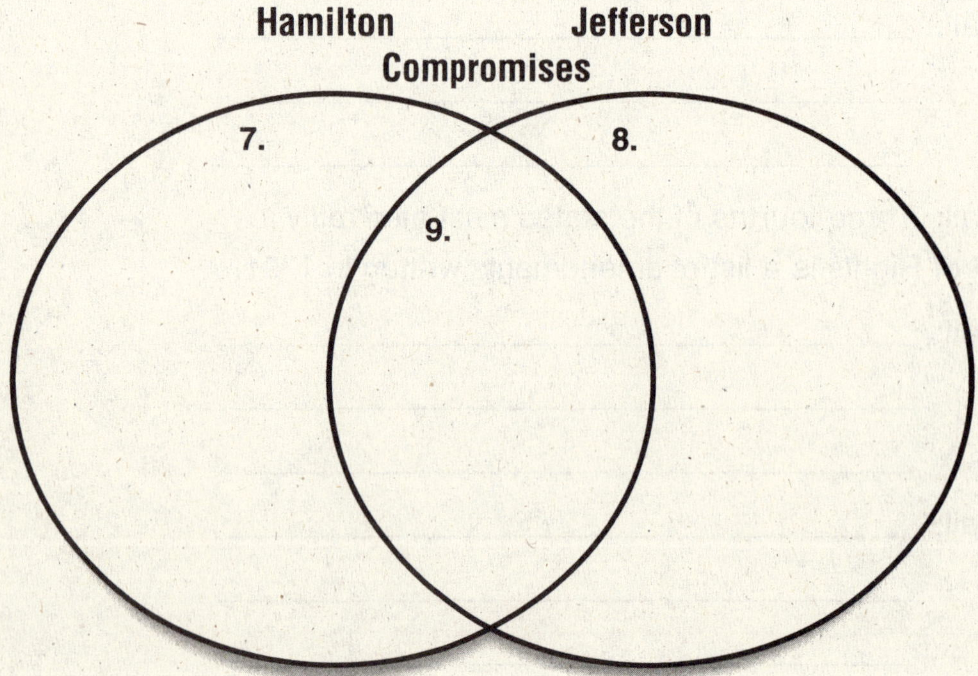

Almanac Map Practice

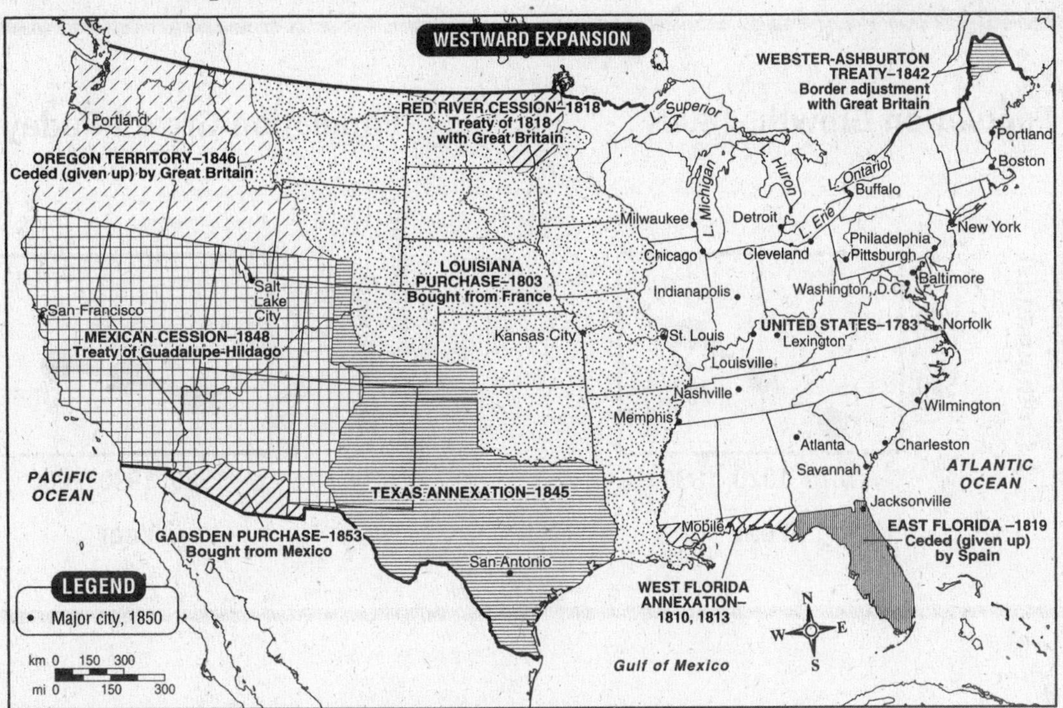

Use the map to do these activities and answer these questions.

Practice

1. Draw a circle around the areas received from Britain.

2. Draw a line connecting the two areas that the United States *bought* from other nations.

3. What were these areas called? From which nations did the United States buy these lands? ____

____

4. In what year did Mexico give up its lands along the Pacific Ocean?

____

Apply

5. Work with a partner to find your state on this map. When did this land become part of the United States? What country claimed the land before it became part of the United States?

____

____

Almanac Graph Practice

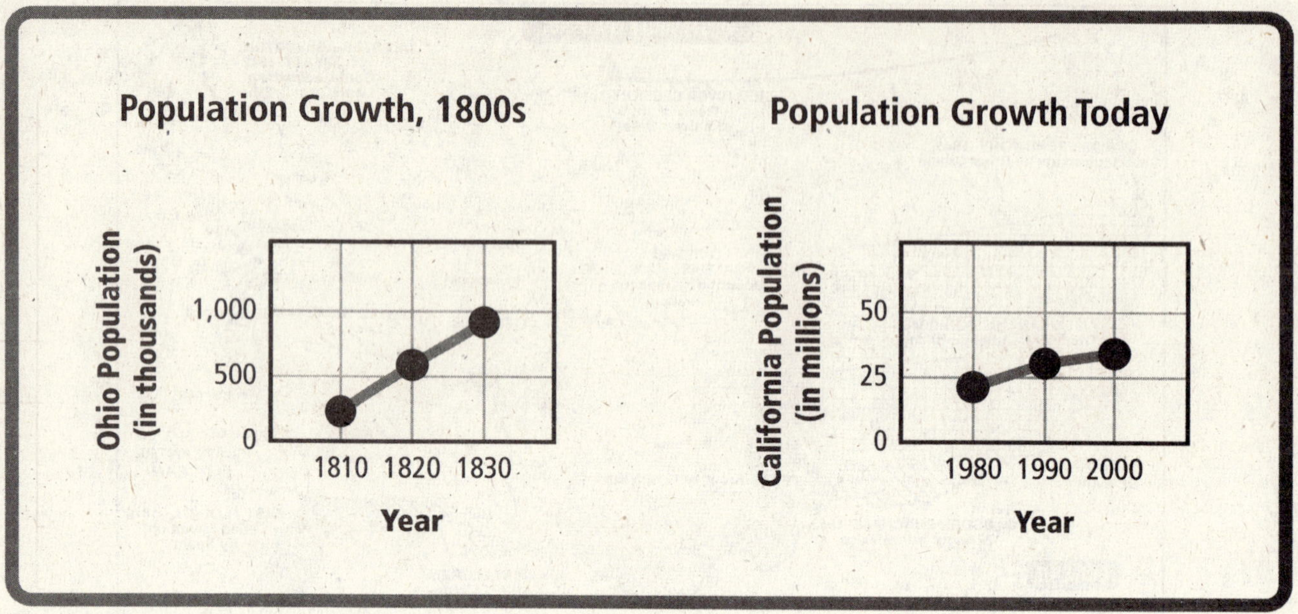

Practice

1. By how much did Ohio's population increase from 1820 to 1830?

____

2. Which state's population increased more during a 20-year period,

Ohio's or California's? ____

Apply

3. Use the information below to complete the line graph.

U.S. Population Aged 65 and Older

Year	Population
1900	3,080,000
1930	6,634,000
1960	16,560,000
1990	31,242,000

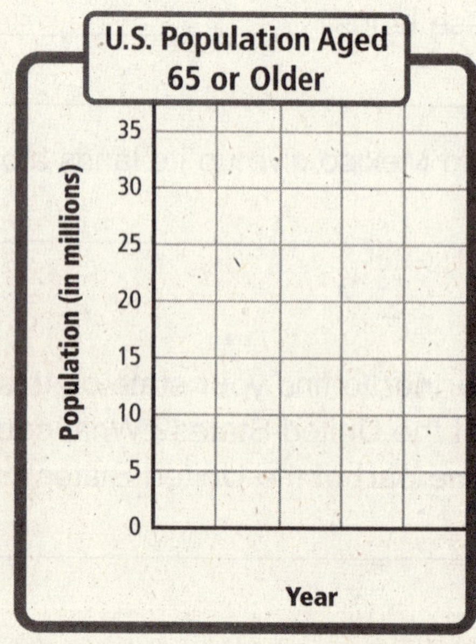

Vocabulary and Study Guide

Vocabulary

Across
1. Daniel Boone was one.
2. These helped settlers travel on rivers.

Down
3. The Erie _____ advanced travel and shipping.
4. Life was often hard here.

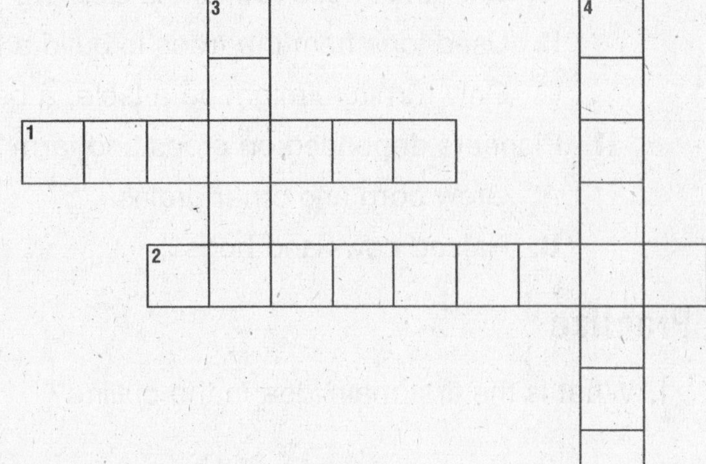

Study Guide

Read "Exploring the Frontier." Then choose the correct ending to each statement below.

5. The first colonists in America settled between the Atlantic Ocean and the

   A. Mississippi River.   **B.** Erie Canal.   **C.** Appalachian Mountains.

6. People tried to cross the Appalachians because the land in the East was

   A. getting full.   **B.** difficult to farm.   **C.** controlled by the king.

7. Daniel Boone helped clear the

   A. Erie Canal.   **B.** Kentucky Trail.   **C.** Wilderness Road.

8. Read "Life on the Frontier." Then fill in the blanks below.

   Thousands of people crossed the _______________ looking for

farmland and _______________. Moving west was often difficult

for settlers, although some were able to travel by river on

_______________. Settlers moved to a region called the

_______________, which was already settled by American Indians.

Settlers and American Indians fought over _______________. They

also borrowed each other's ideas and _______________.

Skillbuilder: Make an Outline

    I. Pioneers on the frontier were eager to build homes.

        A. Cut down trees to make a clearing

        B. Used logs from the trees to build a rough house

        C. Only furniture might be a table, a bed, and a spinning wheel

    II. Pioneers depended on crops and farm animals for food.

        A. Grew corn and other grains

        B. Raised cows and hogs

Practice

1. What is the first main idea in the outline?

____

2. How many supporting details does the second main idea have? _____

3. What title would you give this outline?

____

4. Write an additional detail to support the second main idea.

____

Apply

Create an outline of this passage. Write your outline on a separate sheet of paper.

> By the late 1700s, thousands of settlers had crossed the Appalachian Mountains. They went to the Ohio and Mississippi river valleys looking for good, inexpensive farmland and new opportunities.
>
> As the settlers went west, they moved onto land that was already settled by American Indians. Shawnee, Choctaw, Cherokee, and other American Indian nations built villages, farmed, and hunted between the Appalachians and the Mississippi River. American Indians and settlers fought for this land. They also borrowed each others' ideas and customs.

Use with *United States History*, pp. 352–353

Vocabulary and Study Guide

Vocabulary

1. Draw a line connecting the vocabulary word to its meaning.

corps	A person who helps people understand each other
manufacturer	The place where a river begins
source	A team of people working together
interpreter	A person who uses machines to make goods

Study Guide

Read "President Jefferson." Then answer the questions.

2. To what political party did President Jefferson belong? What did his

party believe? ____

____

3. What country owned the Louisiana Territory? Why did it want to

sell it? ____

Read "Exploring the West." Then answer the questions.

4. Who led the expedition into the Louisiana Territory?

____

5. Did the Corps of Discovery find a water route to the Pacific Ocean?

What did it prove? ____

____

Vocabulary and Study Guide

Vocabulary

Write the word for each definition below.

1. ________________ A deep loyalty to one's country

2. ________________ Having enough food, clothing, and shelter to be comfortable

3. ________________ A government's actions towards other nations

4. Use two of the words in a sentence.

____

____

Study Guide

Read "The War of 1812." Then fill in the classification chart below.

Question	Dolley Madison	Francis Scott Key	James Monroe	Noah Webster
Who am I?	5.	7.	9.	11.
What did I do?	6.	8.	10.	12.

Vocabulary and Study Guide

Vocabulary

Write the definition of each vocabulary word below.

1. campaign ____

2. ruling ____

3. suffrage ____

4. Use the word *campaign* in a sentence about Andrew Jackson's election strategy.

____

____

Study Guide

Read "A New Kind of President." Then fill in the sequence chart below.

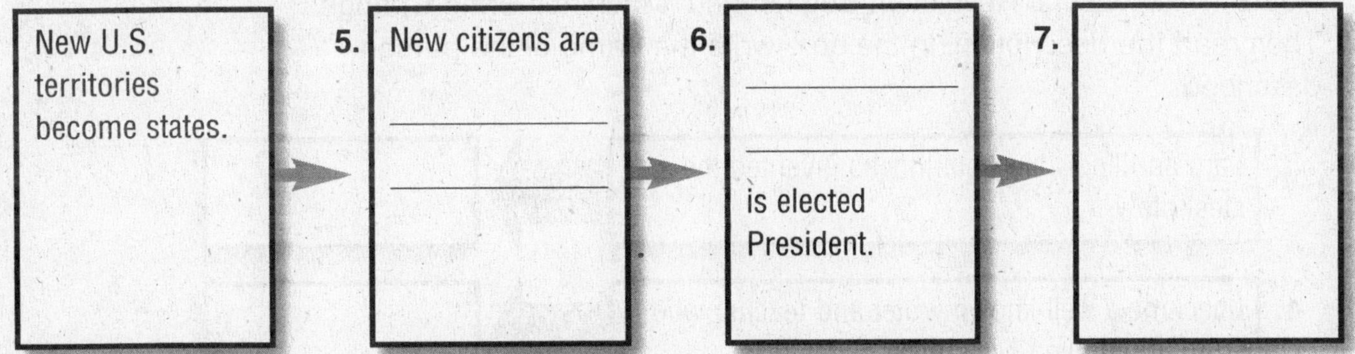

Read "Indian Removal Act." Then fill in the sequence chart below.

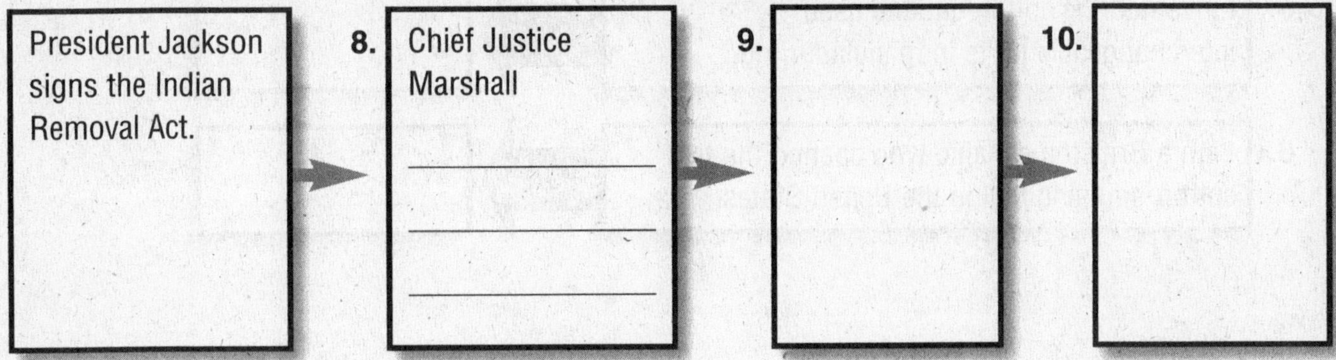

Vocabulary and Study Guide

Vocabulary

1. Use *interchangeable parts, mass production,* and *productivity* in one or

two sentences that show their relationship. _______________________

____

____

2. Use *entrepreneur* and *textile* in a sentence that shows their

relationship. ____

____

____

Study Guide

Read "The Industrial Revolution Begins" and "Machines Bring Change."
Then read the description. In the box, write the name of the person
described.

3. I am an Illinois blacksmith who invented the steel plow. **I am →** [ ]

4. I became a well-known writer and teacher who wrote about the Lowell mills. **I am →** [ ]

5. I invented the cotton gin and used interchangeable parts in manufacturing. **I am →** [ ]

6. I am a British mechanic who opened the first cotton-spinning mill in the United States. **I am →** [ ]

Skillbuilder: Find and Evaluate Sources

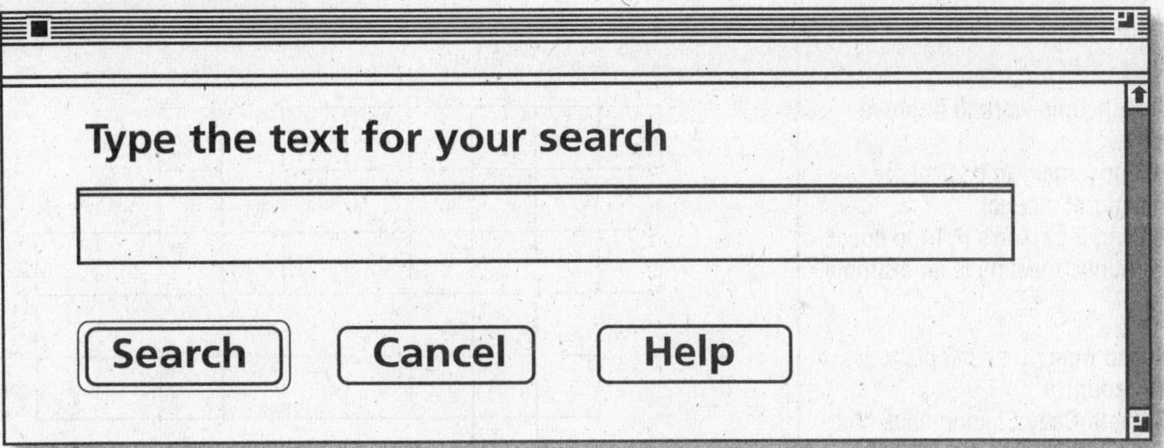

Practice

1. Look at the Internet search window above. Circle the place where you type in your keyword or phrase.

2. If your research question is, "What was the Irish Potato Famine?" what keyword or words would you type? _______________________

3. Which of the two sources shown below would be considered a more reliable source for a research paper? Why?

   An entry in an encyclopedia

   An article in a popular magazine

   ____

   ____

Apply

Start a plan for a research paper about the Irish Potato Famine. Write a question about what you want to research. Then use the Internet and/or the library to find two reliable sources to answer your question. Explain why each resource is a reliable resource.

 Use with *United States History*, pp. 386–387

Vocabulary and Study Guide

Vocabulary

Across

1. When people work to improve society
2. The movement to control the drinking of alcohol
3. Denying a person's right to speak in a public meeting is an example.

Down

4. Caused many Irish people to leave their country
5. Elizabeth Cady Stanton said, "All _____ and women are created equal."

Study Guide

6. Read "German and Irish Immigrants." Then fill in the blanks below.

   Irish and German people came to the United States for job

opportunities and to own land. Thousands of Germans left Europe

because of war and _____________________. Many settled

in the Midwest. Some bought land, and some found work in

_____________________. Many Irish people immigrated because of

the _____________________. Most Irish immigrants settled in the

_____________________.

7. Read "Making a Better Society." Then fill in the blanks below.

   During the Second Great Awakening, people worked to improve

society through _____________________. Many women who worked

in the antislavery movement realized that they also faced

_____________________ as women. Women were not allowed to

vote or own _____________________. In 1848, a group of women led

by Elizabeth Cady Stanton held a convention to talk about these

rights. Stanton and _____________________ worked to change laws.

Vocabulary and Study Guide

Vocabulary

1. Draw a line connecting the vocabulary word to its meaning.

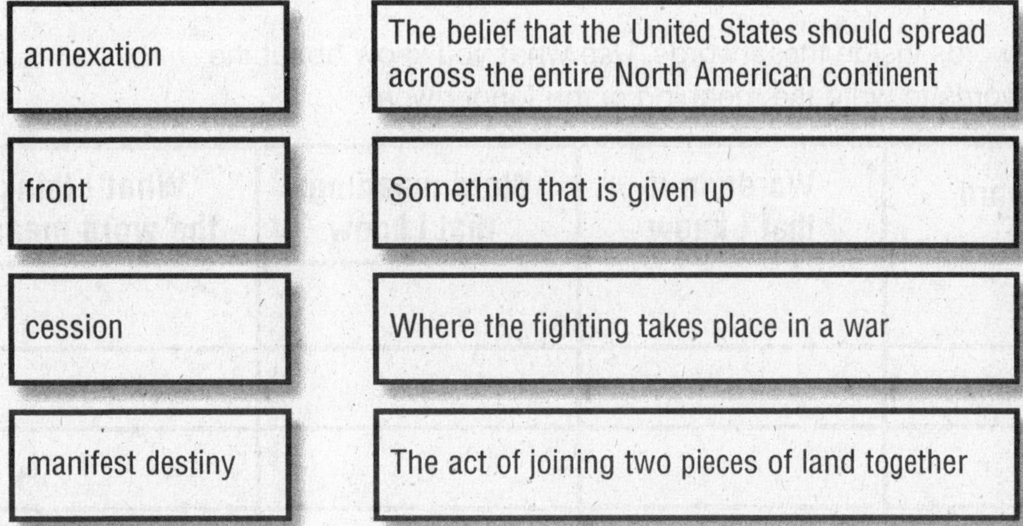

Study Guide

Read "The Texas Revolution." Then fill in the sequence chart below.

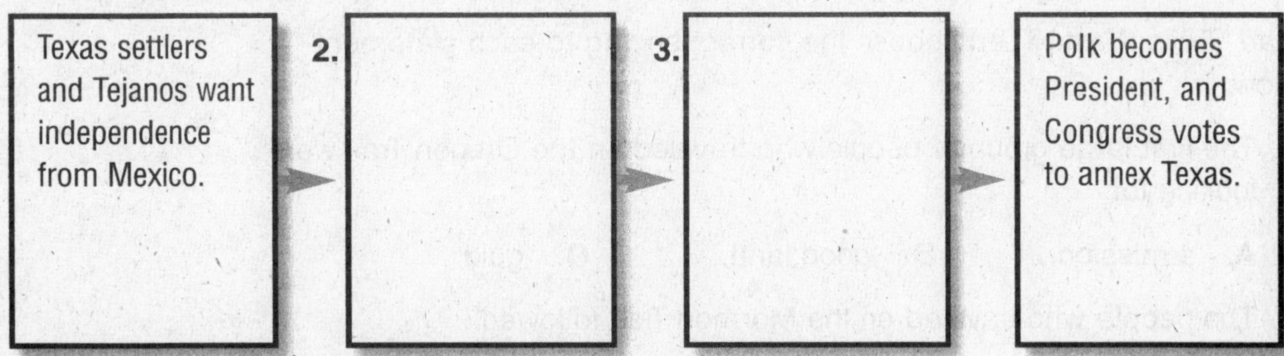

Read "War with Mexico." Then fill in the sequence chart below.

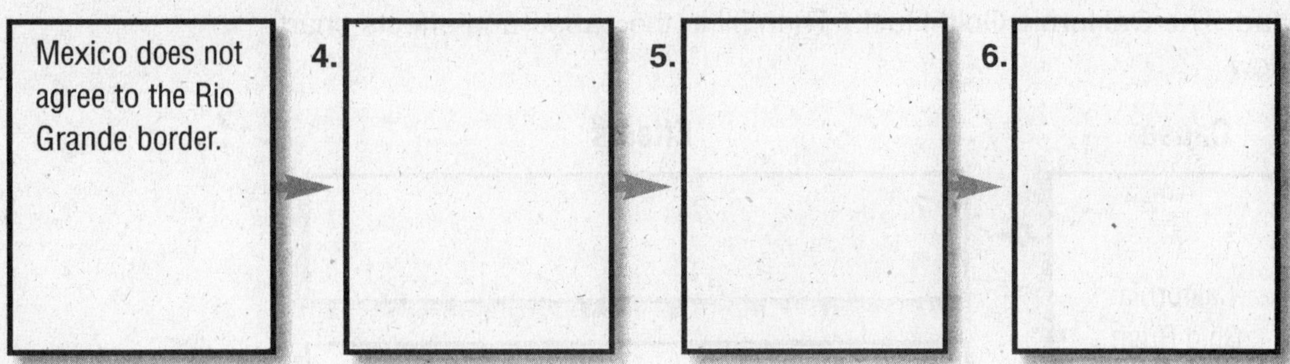

Vocabulary and Study Guide

Vocabulary

If you do not know a word's meaning, try breaking it into smaller parts. It may contain a smaller word that you know.

Find the smaller words inside these words. Use what you know about the smaller word or words to write the meaning of the longer word.

	New word	Words in it that I know	Word meanings that I know	What I think the word means
1.	wagon train			
2.	forty-niner			
3.	gold rush			
4.	boomtown			

Study Guide

Read "Trails West." Then choose the correct ending to each statement below.

5. The first large group of people who traveled on the Oregon Trail were looking for

   A. a mission.   **B.** good land.   **C.** gold.

6. The people who traveled on the Mormon Trail followed

   A. ranchers.   **B.** forty-niners.   **C.** Brigham Young.

Read "The California Gold Rush." Then fill in the cause-and-effects chart below.

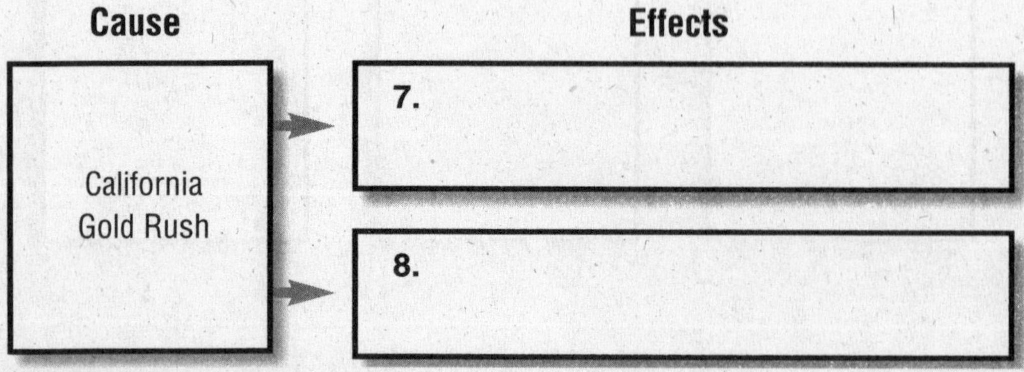

Almanac Map Practice

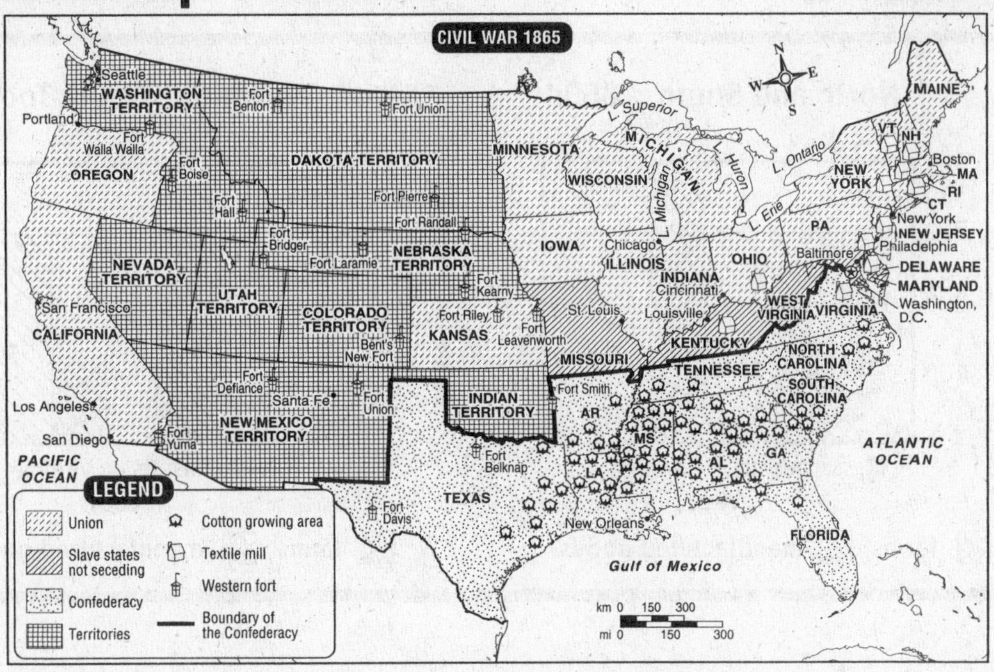

Use the map to do these activities and answer these questions.

Practice

1. Draw a circle around each major city in both the Union and Confederacy.

2. How many major cities does the map show on the Union side? The

   Confederate side? _______________________________________

3. On which side of the Civil War were most cotton producers located?

   Most textile mills? _______________________________________

   ____

Apply

4. Work with a partner. Read about free states and slave states in "Compromises in Congress" in Lesson 3 of Chapter 12.

   Look at the map above. Then explain why Missouri was a slave state, Maine was a free state, and Kansas and Nebraska were given popular sovereignty.

   ____

   ____

Almanac Graph Practice

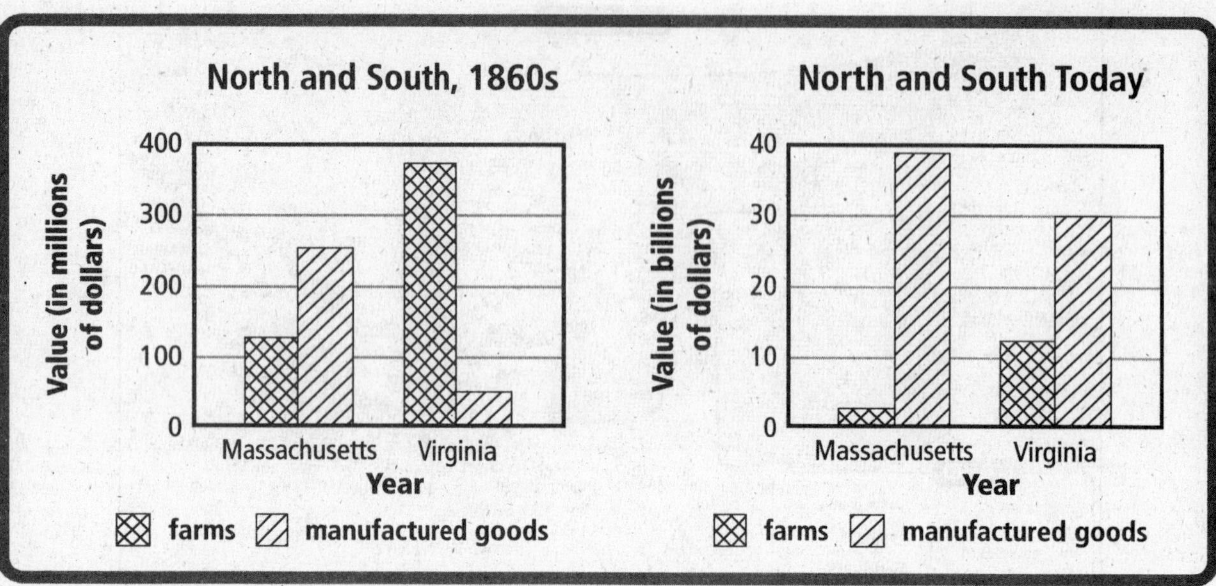

Practice

1. In the 1860s, did southern states such as Virginia rely more on

farming or manufacturing? _________________________________

2. About how many billions of dollars of manufactured goods does

Massachusetts produce today? _________________________________

Apply

3. The information in the chart compares the amount of money people
earned in Massachusetts and Virginia in 1950 and 2000. Use the data
in the chart to complete the double bar graph below.

Personal Income Per Person

State	1950	2000
Massachusetts	1,656	37,960
Virginia	1,257	31,320

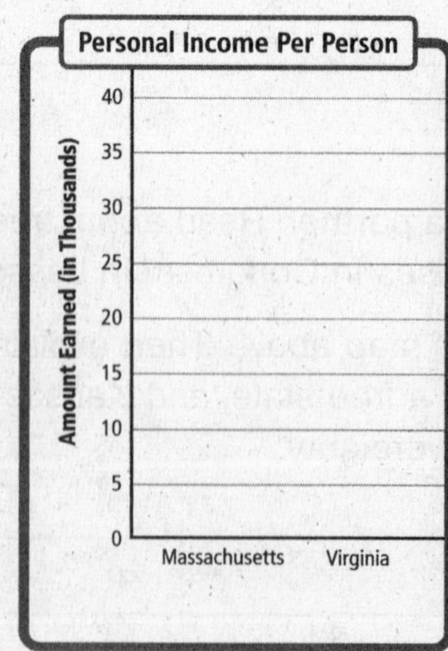

Use with *United States History*, pp. 412–413

Vocabulary and Study Guide

Vocabulary

Write the definition of each vocabulary word below.

1. tariff ____

2. states' rights ____

____

____

3. sectionalism ____

4. Use two of the words in a sentence. __________________

____

____

Study Guide

Read "Slavery in the United States." Then fill in the sequence chart below.

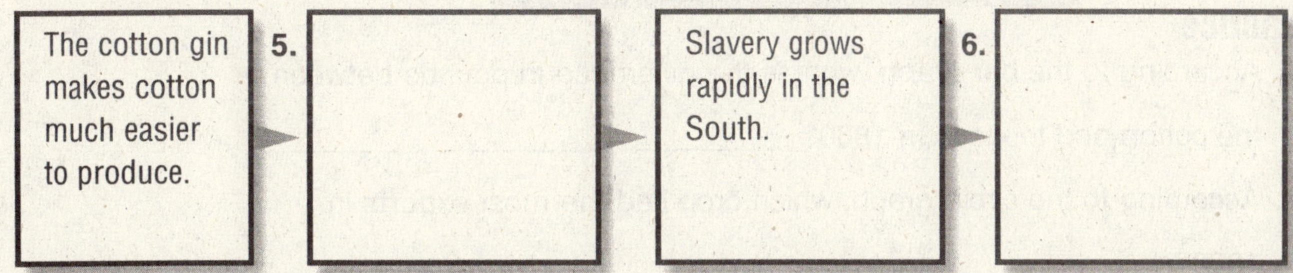

Read "North and South." Then fill in the compare and contrast chart below.

Region	Economy	Products
South	**7.**	**9.**
North	**8.**	**10.**

Skillbuilder: Compare Bar, Line, and Circle Graphs

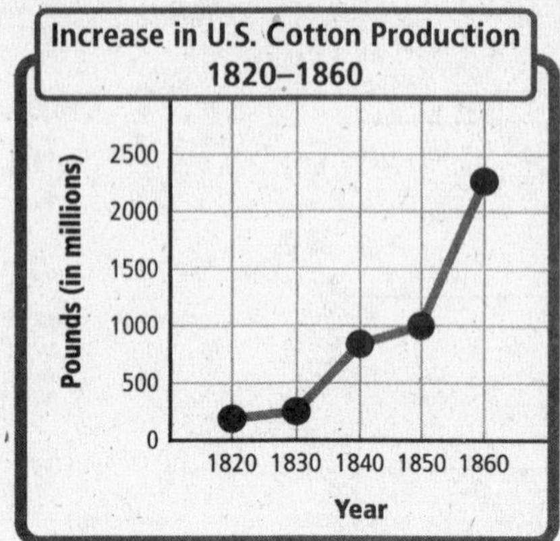

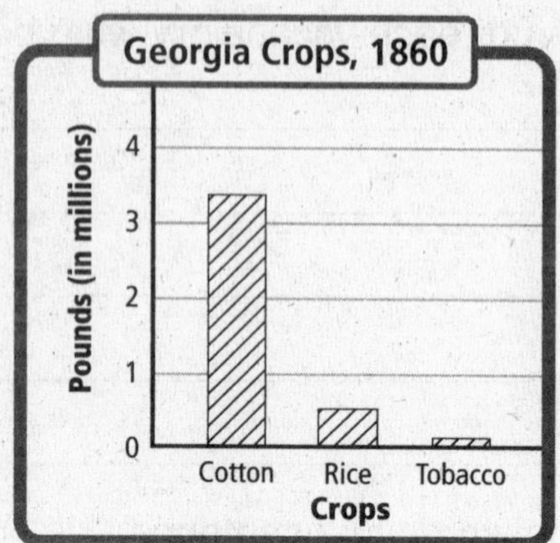

Practice

1. According to the bar graph, what is the difference in pounds between the cotton and tobacco in 1860? _______________________

2. According to the circle graph, which crop had the most exports in 1860? _______________________

3. What is the span of years on the line graph? _______________________

4. How are bar graphs, line graphs, and circle graphs different? _______

____

____

____

Apply

Now use what you know about graphs to redraw the graphs. Draw a bar graph to show that the same amount of rice and tobacco were produced in 1860. Draw a line graph to show that cotton production decreased steadily from 1800 to 1860. Then draw a circle graph to show that the same amount of cotton, tobacco, and wheat was exported.

Use with *United States History*, pp. 422–423

Vocabulary and Study Guide

Vocabulary

When you add a suffix to the end of a base word, you make a new word. Knowing a suffix and its base word can help you understand unfamiliar words. Look at the word *conductor*.

> Conduct "to lead or to guide"
> +
> -or "one who does a certain thing"
> =
> Conductor "one who leads or guides"

Break down the vocabulary word into its base word and suffix. Write the meaning of the new word.

> -ist "one who does something"
> -tion "the act of"
> -ism "the practice of"

1. Abolitionist = ____ + _______

Abolitionist means ____

2. Discrimination = ______________________________________ + _______

Discrimination means ______________________________________

3. Sectionalism = ___________________________________ + _______

Sectionalism means ____

Study Guide

4. Read "The Antislavery Movement." Then match these people to their identities by drawing a line between the name and the identity.

William Lloyd Garrison	printed antislavery newspaper, *The Liberator*
Frederick Douglass	spoke for abolition and women's rights
Sojourner Truth	spoke to white audiences about slavery

Vocabulary and Study Guide

Vocabulary

1. Draw a line connecting the vocabulary word to its meaning.

Study Guide

Read "Would Slavery Spread?" Then fill in the main idea and details chart below.

Compromise	What it did
Missouri Compromise	**2.**
Compromise of 1850	**3.**
Kansas-Nebraska Act	**4.**

Read "The Growing Crisis." Then answer the question.

5. What are three events that increased tension between the North and South?

____

____

Vocabulary and Study Guide

Vocabulary

Across

1. Eleven southern states left the Union and formed the _______.
2. What southerners called for to protect their right to own enslaved people
3. Said to the South, "We are not enemies, but friends"
4. An issue dividing the North and South

Down

1. Began with the attack on Fort Sumter
2. President of the Confederate States

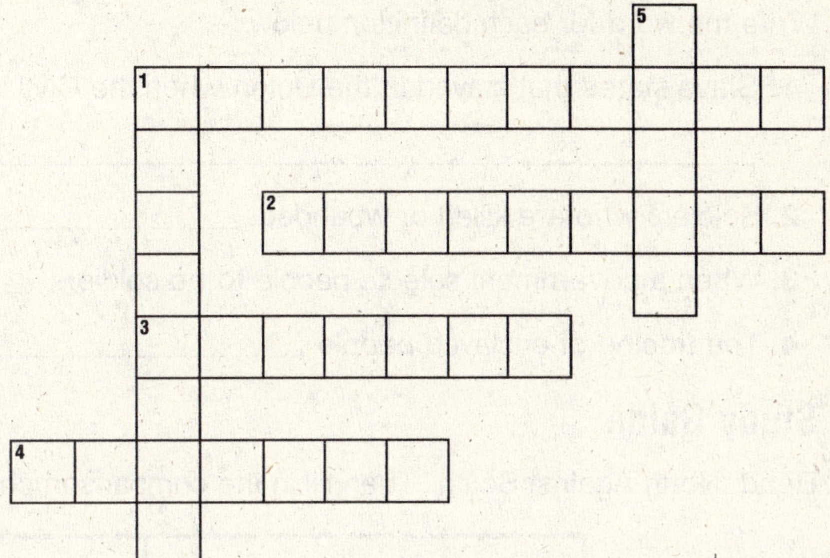

Study Guide

6. Read "Abraham Lincoln" and "Lincoln's Campaigns." Then fill in the blanks below.

Abraham Lincoln was born in _________________, but his family moved to _________________ when he was a boy. Lincoln studied and became a successful _________________. He was a member of the _________________ Party. He also became a member of the Illinois legislature and later served one term in the _________________. Lincoln argued against the spread of slavery, but he did not call for _________________.

7. Read "Secession Begins." Then fill in the blanks below.

Seven southern states decided to leave the Union and form the _________________ States of America. The South Carolina state militia surrounded _________________, which had U.S. soldiers inside. When President Lincoln sent _________________ to the fort, the Confederacy fired on the fort with cannons. This was the start of the _________________.

Vocabulary and Study Guide

Vocabulary

Write the word for each definition below.

1. Slave states that stayed in the Union when the Civil War began

   ____

2. Soldiers who are killed or wounded _________________________________

3. When a government selects people to be soldiers _________________

4. The freeing of enslaved people _________________________________

Study Guide

Read "North Against South." Then fill in the comparison chart below.

	Advantages	**Strategies**
Union	Larger population; More factories and railroad lines	5.
Confederacy	6.	7.

8. Read "The War's Leaders" and "Turning Points." Then fill in the blanks below.

   At the start of the Civil War, President Lincoln did not plan

   to _________________________________ enslaved people. Then

   Lincoln issued the _________________________________ to weaken

   the Confederacy. After that, the Civil War became a war to end

   _________________________________. In 1863, the Union won an

   important battle at _________________________________ and gained

   full control of the Mississippi River. The Union also won the Battle

   of Gettysburg, where President Lincoln later made a famous speech

   called the _________________________________.

Vocabulary and Study Guide

Vocabulary

Write the definition of each vocabulary word below.

1. camp ____

2. home front ____

____

3. Use the words in a sentence. ____

____

____

Study Guide

Read "The Soldier's Life." Then fill in the Venn diagram below.

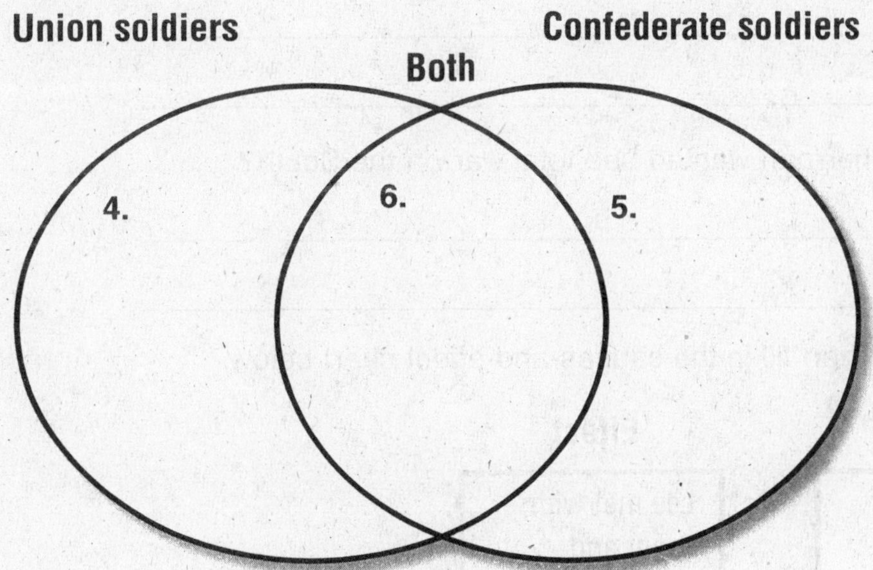

Read "On the Home Front." Then answer the questions.

7. Why did people in the North need photographs to understand camp life and battles?

____

8. Why was life especially hard in the South during the war?

____

Vocabulary and Study Guide

Vocabulary

Write the definition of each vocabulary word below.

1. telegraph ____

____

2. total war ____

____

3. desert ____

Study Guide

Read "Union Victories." Then answer the questions.

4. What two Union victories further weakened the Confederacy?

____

____

5. Why did General Sherman want to use total war on the South?

____

____

Read "Grant and Lee." Then fill in the causes-and-effect chart below.

Causes	**Effect**
6.	Lee met with Grant and agreed to surrender.
7.	

Vocabulary and Study Guide

Vocabulary

Across

1. Murder of an important leader
2. To charge a government official with a crime

Down

3. _____ Republicans
4. During Reconstruction, the South _____ the Union.
5. Southern states passed the Black _____.

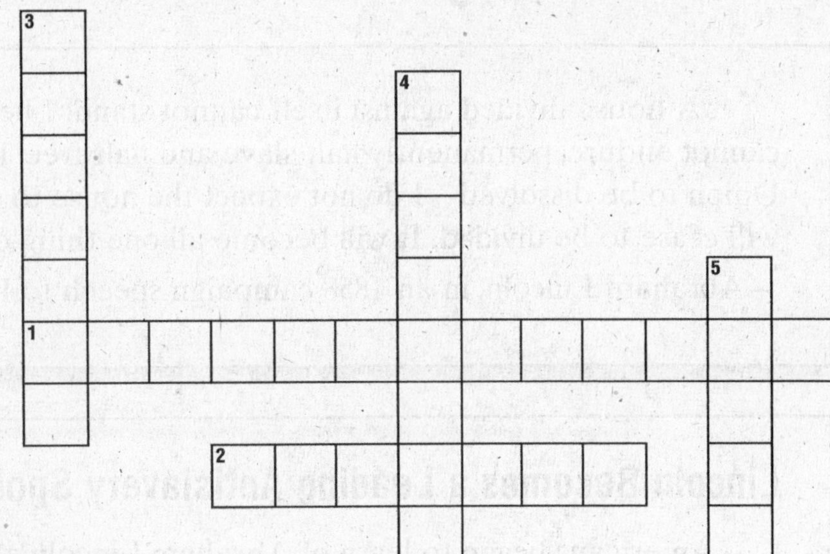

Study Guide

6. Read "Plans for Reconstruction" and "Reconstruction." Then fill in the blanks below.

   Before a plan for Reconstruction was agreed upon, President Lincoln was _______________________. _______________________ became President. Radical Republicans became upset because of the South's _______________________ and the election of former _______________________ leaders to Congress. Congress took control of Reconstruction, put the South under military rule, and voted to _______________________ the President.

7. Read "The Constitution Changes." Then fill in the blanks below.

   Congress created the 13th, 14th, and 15th _______________________ to protect the rights of _______________________. These amendments gave the national government more power over the states. African Americans were granted full _______________________ and the right to fair and equal treatment. Some African American men became government leaders.

Skillbuilder: Compare Primary and Secondary Sources

> "A house divided against itself cannot stand. I believe this government cannot endure, permanently half slave and half free. I do not expect the Union to be dissolved—I do not expect the house to fall—but I do expect it will cease to be divided. It will become all one thing or all the other."
>
> —Abraham Lincoln, in an 1858 campaign speech to Illinois Republicans

Lincoln Becomes a Leading Antislavery Spokesperson

Americans began to learn of Abraham Lincoln's views on slavery when he challenged Stephen Douglas in the 1858 Illinois Senate election. Lincoln did not speak to outlaw slavery in the South, but he did not think the country could continue to be half slave states and half free states. He believed that soon the country would have to become all slave or all free states.

Practice

1. Is Abraham Lincoln's speech a primary or secondary source? How do you know? ____

2. What facts do the two sources share? _______________________

____

____

3. What do you learn from the passage that you do not learn from

Lincoln's speech? ____

____

Apply

Find a book that is an example of a primary source. Then find a book that is an example of a secondary source. On a separate sheet of paper, write a paragraph explaining how you identified each one.

Name _______________________ Date _______________

Vocabulary and Study Guide

Vocabulary

Write the definition of each vocabulary word below.

1. sharecropping ____

____

____

2. Jim Crow ____

____

3. segregation ____

4. Use two of the words in a sentence.

____

____

____

Study Guide

Read "Freedom and Hardship." Then fill in the causes-and-effects chart below.

Causes	Effects
Many African Americans became sharecroppers.	**5.**
6.	They formed the Ku Klux Klan.

Name _________________________________ Date _____________

Almanac Map Practice

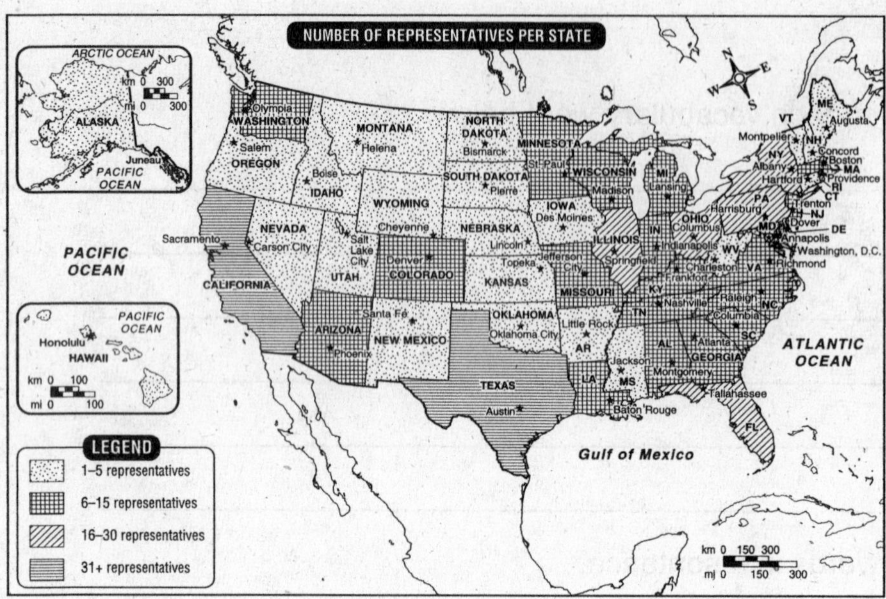

Use the map to do these activities and answer these questions.

Practice

1. How many representatives does Ohio have? _________________________

2. Which state has more representatives, South Carolina or Hawaii?

   ____

3. Which state bordering the Gulf of Mexico has 5 or fewer

   representatives? ____

4. Describe how West Virginia is different from the other states near it.

   ____

   ____

Apply

5. Work with a partner to locate the states that have the highest
   numbers of representatives. Then discuss the following question and
   provide an answer to it: Why do you think the states with the highest
   number of representatives are all located along major waterways?

   ____

   ____

   ____

Almanac Graph Practice

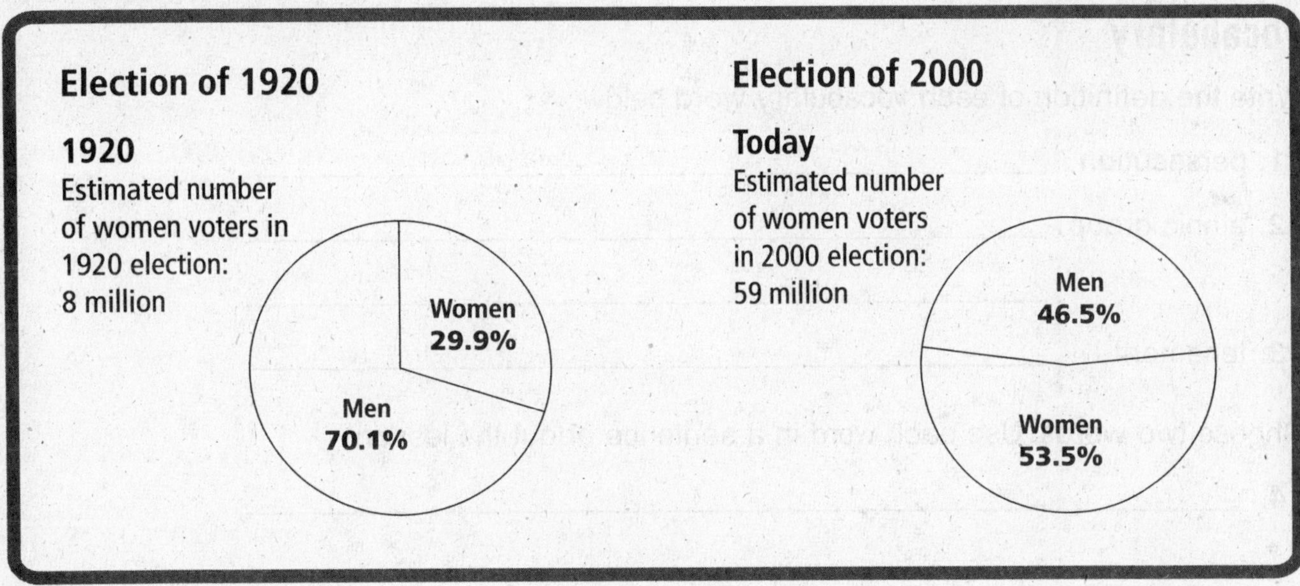

Practice

1. How many women voted in the election in 1920? _______________

2. How did the number of women voters change from 1920 to 2000?

____

Apply

3. Use the information below to complete the pie graphs.

- **1920 Presidential Election**

  Harding: 60.3% of the popular vote
  Cox: 34.1% of the popular vote
  Other: 5.6% of the popular vote

- **2000 Presidential Election**

  Gore: 48.4% of the popular vote
  Bush: 47.9% of the popular vote
  Other: 3.7% of the popular vote

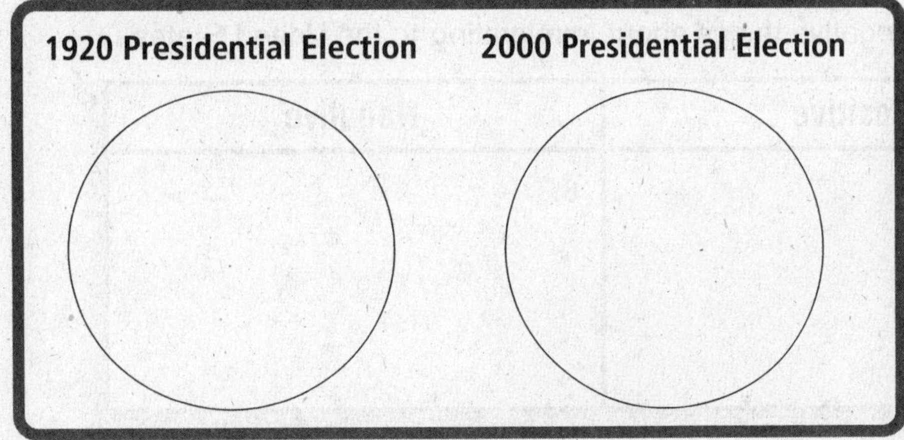

Vocabulary and Study Guide

Vocabulary

Write the definition of each vocabulary word below.

1. persecution ____

2. ethnic group ____

____

3. tenement ____

Choose two words. Use each word in a sentence about the lesson.

4. ____

____

5. ____

____

Study Guide

6. Read "Coming to America." Then fill in the blanks below.

Most new immigrants to the United States between 1880 and

1920 came from _______________________ Europe. Immigrants

usually entered the country through immigration stations such as

_______________________ in New York City. Immigrants from China

flocked to _______________________ to search for gold.

Read "Living in a New Country." Then fill in the classification chart below
with positive and negative things about immigrating to the United States.

Positive	Negative
7.	8.

Vocabulary and Study Guide

Vocabulary

Read the clue and write the answer in the blank. Then find the word in the
puzzle. Look up, down, forward, and backward.

1. The maximum number of people allowed to enter a country ___________

2. People fleeing danger in their home countries ___________

3. Temporary farm workers from Mexico ___________

4. A person who enters a new country to live there permanently ___________

A	Y	I	Q	U	R	T	O
Z	C	M	B	R	E	F	G
M	N	M	O	E	X	A	H
L	M	I	B	F	R	K	U
E	S	G	T	U	S	Q	J
I	I	R	P	G	U	U	K
B	R	A	C	E	R	O	S
Q	U	N	T	E	A	T	L
E	A	T	A	S	B	A	O

Study Guide

Read "Limiting Immigration." Then fill in the sequence chart below.

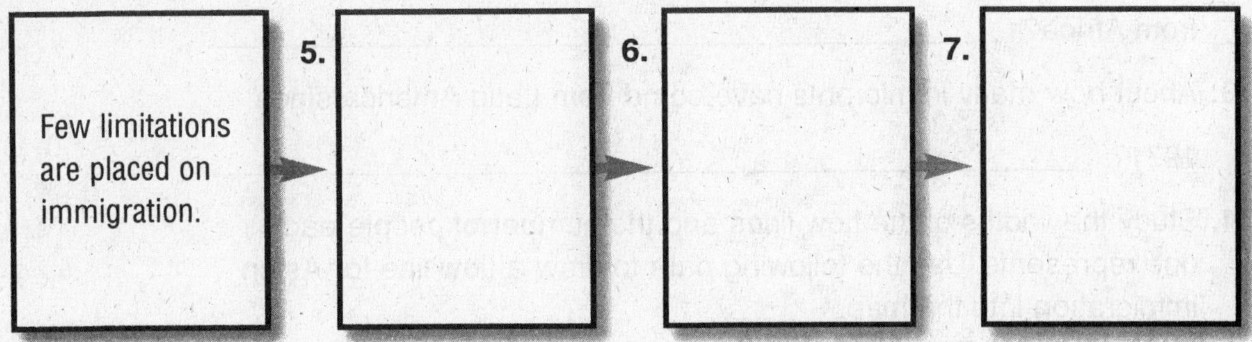

8. Read "A New Era of Immigration." Then write about the Vietnamese refugees.

____

____

____

Skillbuilder: Read Flow Lines on a Map

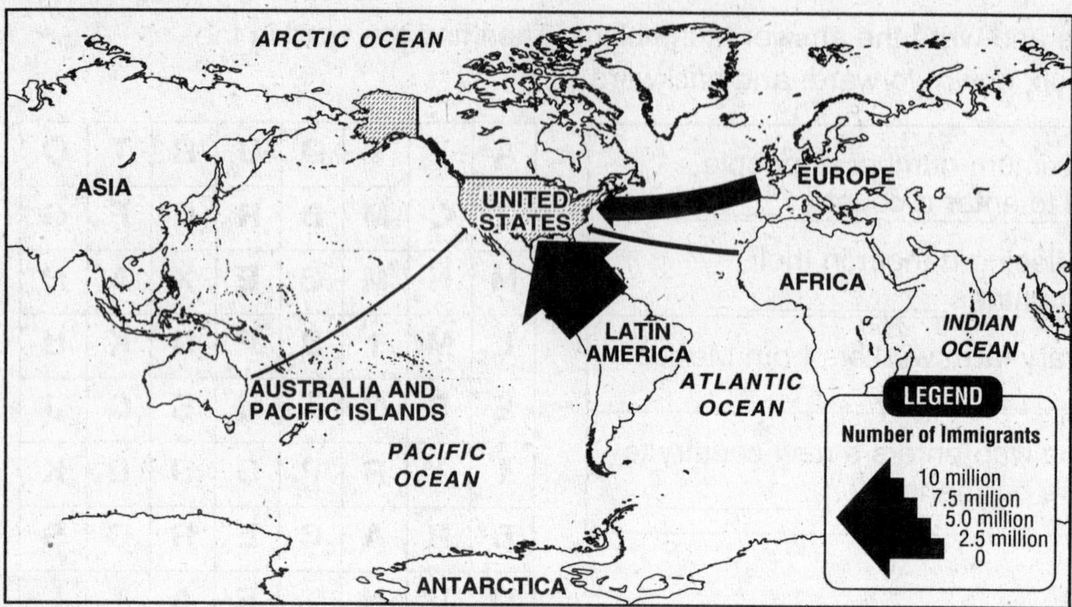

Practice

1. From what region on the map have the fewest immigrants come?

____

2. Have more people immigrated to the United States from Europe or

from Africa? _______________________________

3. About how many immigrants have come from Latin America since

1971? _______________________________

4. Study the widths of the flow lines and the number of people each
one represents. Use the following data to draw a flow line for Asian
immigration into the map.

Asian Immigration, 1971–2000

7,122,007

Apply

Find or create a world map. Using the data below, turn the map into a flow
line map. Be sure to draw a legend for the map.

U.S. Immigration, 1850s

Ireland 160,000	Great Britain 50,000
Germany 80,000	Canada 10,000

Name _________________________ Date _________

Vocabulary and Study Guide

Vocabulary

Read the clue and unscramble the letters to write the correct word.

1. Something handed down from past generations.

| T | A | E | H | E | I | R | G | _________________

2. A short statement that explains an ideal.

| O | M | O | T | T | _________________

3. Unfair treatment toward a group of people.

| S | M | I | N | I | A | D | I | C | O | N | T | R | I | _________________

Study Guide

Read "Many People, One Nation." Then choose the correct ending to each statement below.

4. Almost one-third of immigrants to the United States are from

   A. Canada.   **B.** China.   **C.** Latin America.

5. Each ethnic group adds new language, food, and

   A. customs.   **B.** money.   **C.** transportation.

6. The word *kindergarten* is originally a word in

   A. French.   **B.** German.   **C.** Japanese.

Read "Our Shared Values." Then fill in the cause in the chart below.

Cause	Effect
7.	Rights have been extended to more Americans.

Name _______________________________ Date ______________

Vocabulary and Study Guide

Vocabulary

1. Draw a line connecting the vocabulary word to its meaning.

prejudice	A person who takes action for social change
suffragist	An unfair negative opinion about a group
activist	A person who works for the right to vote

Study Guide

2. Read "The Fight for Women's Rights." Then fill in the outline below.

I. Main Idea: ____

    A. Supporting Idea: The suffrage movement

        1. Detail: ____

        ____

        2. Detail: ____

        ____

    B. Supporting Idea: Women gain the right to vote

        1. Detail: ____

        ____

        2. Detail: ____

        ____

3. Read "African American Rights." Then write two methods the NAACP used to gain equality for African Americans.

____

____

____

Vocabulary and Study Guide

Vocabulary

As you read the lesson, fill in the word web with groups that fought for
their civil rights.

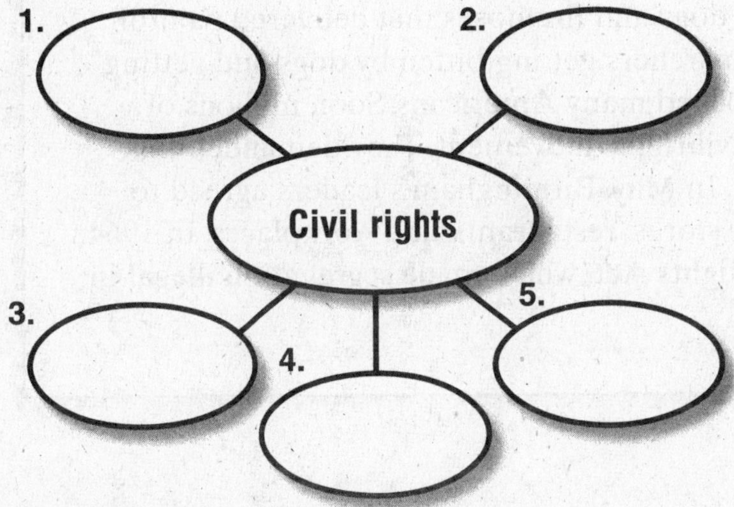

Write the definition of the term below.

6. nonviolent protest ____

____

Study Guide

Read "The Struggle Continues." Then read the description. In the box,
write the name of the person described.

7. I helped start the National Organization for Women. **I am** →

8. I would not give up my seat on the bus. **I am** →

9. I made speeches and helped migrant workers to organize. **I am** →

10. I led the bus boycott in Montgomery, Alabama. **I am** →

Skillbuilder: Resolve Conflicts

In April 1963, Martin Luther King Jr. led protests against segregation in Birmingham, Alabama. More than 1,000 African American young people followed him. The Birmingham police met the protesters with snarling dogs and fire hoses that delivered painful blasts of water. Pictures of marchers getting bitten by dogs and getting knocked down by water shocked many Americans. Soon millions of Americans supported the civil rights movement. They demanded that the government take action. In May, Birmingham's leaders agreed to end segregation in the city's stores, restaurants, and workplaces. In 1964, Congress passed the Civil Rights Act, which made segregation illegal in all 50 states.

Practice

1. What did the African Americans who marched in Birmingham want?

____

2. Did the government of Birmingham feel the same way as the marchers? How do you know? _______________________

____

3. What was the result of this conflict in Birmingham?

____

____

4. How did the U.S. government show that it agreed with the marchers' demands for civil rights? _______________________

____

Apply

Think about a time you had a disagreement with a friend. Write a paragraph describing the disagreement you had. How did you eventually resolve the conflict? Did you both change the way you were feeling?

Vocabulary and Study Guide

Vocabulary

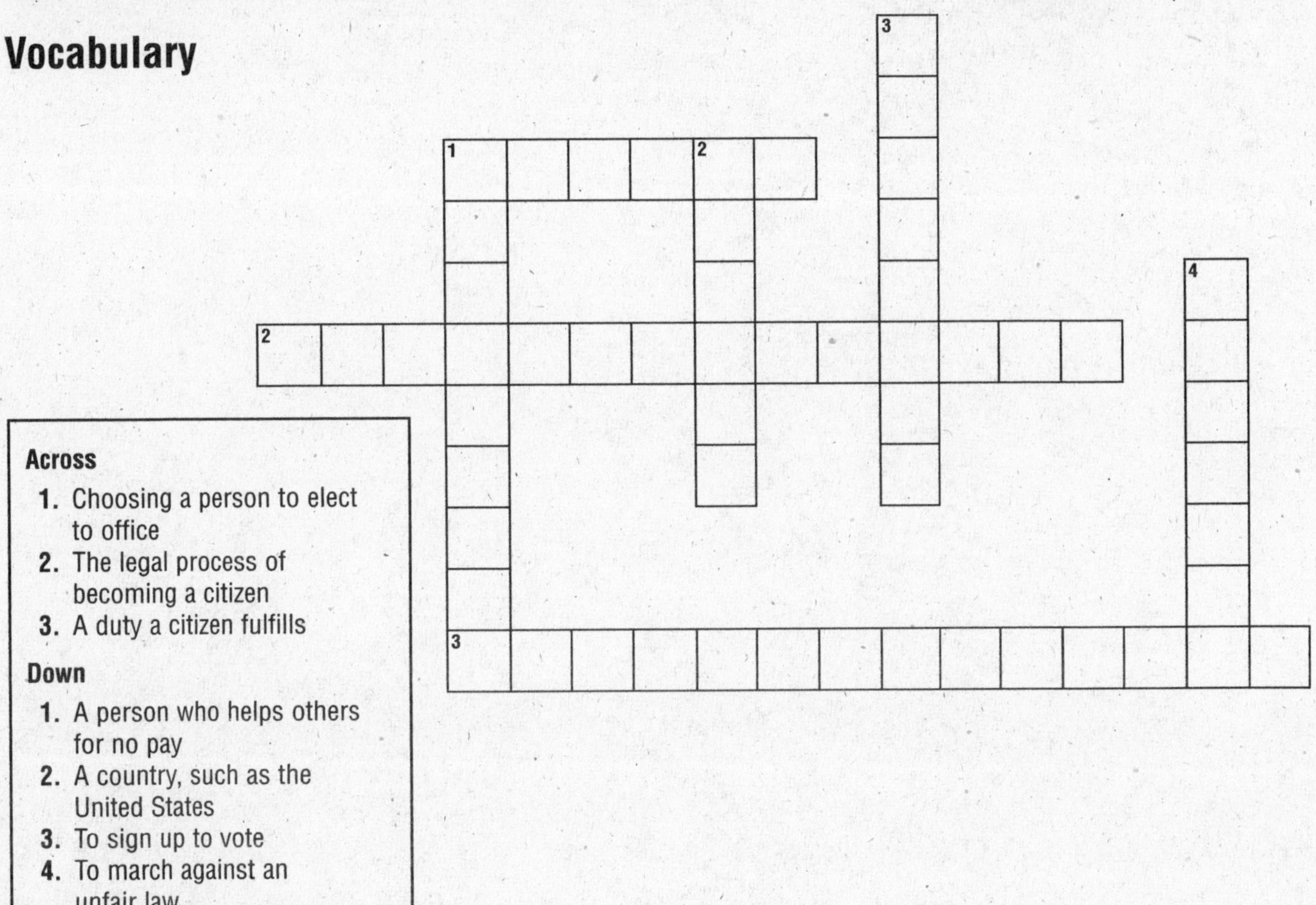

Across

1. Choosing a person to elect to office
2. The legal process of becoming a citizen
3. A duty a citizen fulfills

Down

1. A person who helps others for no pay
2. A country, such as the United States
3. To sign up to vote
4. To march against an unfair law

Study Guide

Read "Citizenship." Then fill in the chart below to explain when these three groups gained full citizenship and the right to vote.

African Americans	Women	American Indians
5.	Gained right to vote in 1920	6.

Read "Responsibilities of Citizens." Then fill in the effect in the chart below.

Cause		Effect
Organizations in Georgia need computers.	→ 7.